Change Success

Change Success

HOW TO MAXIMIZE YOUR PROBABILITY OF SUCCESS IN BOTH ORGANIZATIONAL AND PERSONAL CHANGE

Dr. Chris Mason

ISBN-13: 9780648553205

Library of Congress Control Number:
LCCN Imprint Name: Melbourne, Victoria, Australia

Table of Contents

Introduction—

THE DECISION TO DO A full-blown research project on change was triggered when I heard that a business friend of mine had taken his own life. Like many of his friends, I immediately wondered what I could have done to prevent this. Around this time, I was reaching the end of my PhD coursework in industrial and organizational psychology and was looking for a research topic. My initial reading included proof that, on average, most change initiatives such as growing a business, improving profitability, or implementing a new piece of technology only have a 30 percent probability of implementation success. On reflecting about my friend, I realized that it was likely that he had given up on life after several failed attempts to fix his business, each time with only a 30 percent probability of success. This trial-and-error process eventually works for most people, but at what cost?

I pondered how to come up with a way to significantly improve the 30 percent probability of success statistic. I thought about the very high cost in both financial and personal terms that occurs with a 70 percent failure rate. Continuously failing destroys confidence and the willingness to persevere under duress. Once I began my initial research, I found evidence that there had been little change in management theory since the 1970s, which suggested that the current practices were more a gradual evolution of thinking rather than a meaningful revolution. That is management by trial and error! Contemporary change management studies seem to focus on the reasons for the failures and not on the development of a new change model. So the decision to research organizational change success was made.

I found research on organizations that suggested a link between the change readiness of an organization and the successful implementation of change. Change readiness is a multilevel construct covering individuals, workgroups, and organizations. Even though implementing organizational change initiatives is one of the most important activities of an organization, it is typical to use the trial-and-error approach, which contributes to the low 30 percent probability of success of change initiatives. I wondered about concepts such as change intentions, change behavior, and resistance to change. In mid-2013, I concluded that organizational leaders lacked guidance and a model that could be used with confidence to successfully implement change. This lack of guidance results in significant waste, the demise of organizations, and a lack of predictability of organizational performance. This problem impacts all organizations regardless of size. I can't imagine any business leader being happy with only a 30 percent probability of the success of any change initiative. The challenge then became how to increase this to an 80 percent probability of success.

The environment in which leaders are attempting to implement change has undergone an accelerated rate of change over the last twenty years. Disruption due to a number of factors, such as globalization and technology, has added further barriers to change. The resultant change fatigue causes stagnation in the implementation process. The increased evidence and visibility of change failures causes hesitation and uncertainty in the minds of leaders. Improved communication, particularly with fast-paced social media, often results in leaders feeling inadequate and unable to keep pace with their peers. The fake news encourages leaders to attempt change in spite of their reservations, resulting in a high-risk trial-and-error methodology that leads to failure on most occasions.

The research methodology I chose for the organizational change success issue is known as a sequential explanatory mixed methods study, which meant that I conducted two studies—a quantitative and a qualitative study—so that I could triangulate the data. In this way I could be confident of any new model that resulted from my research. I proposed to test the relationship between change intentions and organizational change success and between change readiness and organizational change success and then test how these constructs could be used to predict the change success in organizations operating in Australia, United States, and the United Kingdom. I was particularly interested in what makes some leaders more successful in implementing an organizational change initiative than the average leader.

At the time of writing this book, it has been almost six years since the initial research, plenty of time to develop the model and apply it in a variety of scenarios. Having a checklist of key factors that a leader can use to enhance their people, strategies, and plans has had a positive impact on their probability of success. Part A of this book covers the change success model for organizations, explains each of the change factors (of which there are ten) in detail, and shows how to apply these factors in real-life situations. The practical guidelines cover things like auditing the *now* position with regard to a change initiative against a maximum *where* score, identifying the key issues where the biggest gaps are, implementing a series of strategies to boost your score and minimize the gap, measuring your progress, and in the end, maximizing the probability of your success with the change initiative. I provide access to a diagnostic that enables readers to self-assess where they are currently in terms of change success potential and then to do a gap analysis to find what needs to be done to achieve a potential change success probability of 80 percent, which is an indication of a very high probability of success.

In 2018, we reviewed the results from our regular annual survey of hundreds of business advisers and business owners / managers. In these survey results, it became apparent that the increased pace of change and the complexity of issues within an organization caused a significant amount of stress and change fatigue to employees. We decided to conduct another formal research program, this time on personal change success. We knew that the core constructs would still apply, but we expected that the key factors would be different. Our assumption was that, as is with the organizational change success probability, no one would be satisfied with only a 30 percent probability of success for any personal change initiative, such as losing weight, becoming a better leader, or learning a new skill. The challenge was then to determine what someone could do to ensure an 80 percent probability of success with a personal change initiative.

In early 2019 we completed the research and found that some people were significantly more successful than others when it came to a personal change initiative and that they used specific factors to achieve that success. The data suggested that there were nine specific factors to personal change success. We built a second diagnostic to enable individuals to identify the gaps in these nine key success factors for personal change success, and we have included access to this diagnostic as well within this book. Part B of the book follows the structure of Part A but covers the change success model for individuals. If you are more interested in personal change success, you can jump straight to Part B.

In summary, this book covers both organizational (Part A) and personal (Part B) change success, lists the key success factors required to achieve an 80 percent probability of success for each, and shows how any gaps in these factors can be overcome. My intent is to share with you the keys to change success whether you are a leader in an organization or someone desiring more success in life (or both).

Part A—Organizational Change Success

To improve is to change; to be perfect is to change often.

— *Winston Churchill*

The structure of Part A is to provide an overview in the form of an executive summary of the topic, a brief explanation of the research methodology (for those who are interested), a brief overview of the research literature around organizational change, the change model that we developed, and a detailed explanation of the ten change success factors. Using a case study methodology, the use of the diagnostic is demonstrated and then the implementation of a change initiative is explained. This leads to other considerations such as measuring your progress, the impact of organizational change beliefs, barriers to change, and then a question-and-answer section. Using the contents page, you can go straight to any section of specific interest; however, you may find you learn more by investing in reading Part A from beginning to end.

Organizational Change Executive Summary

Change is inevitable. Change is constant.

— *Benjamin Disraeli*

Researchers of change management have established that the average probability of success of implementing an organizational change initiative is only 30 percent (Armenakis & Harris, 2009).[1] Much of the current research is focused on the reasons for the failure of change initiatives rather than what can be done to be more successful. In late 2013, I decided to research how some leaders were able to achieve an organizational change success probability of around 80 percent. This research was conducted in Australia, the United States of America, and the United Kingdom using around 240 leaders as data sources. The research was completed in late 2014.

Three core factors were identified that resulted in a high probability success when applied by the exemplar leaders. These were change readiness, capability, and beliefs. Change readiness and beliefs each contributed 30 percent to the probability of success, and capability accounted for the remaining 40 percent. A total of ten distinct factors for a new

1 Armenakis, A. A., & Harris, S. G. (2009). Reflections: Our journey in organizational change research and practice. *Journal of Change Management, 9*(2), 127-142. doi:10.1080/14697010902879079

organizational change success model were discovered. A diagnostic to aid leaders in estimating their current probability of success with an organizational change initiative was developed to support this new model. This diagnostic enabled leaders to identify specific gaps in their implementation plans that, when bridged through targeted strategies and actions, increased change success probability to at least 80 percent.

This book outlines the research process used to develop the organizational change success model, describes in detail the model and its component parts, suggests ways of improving each of the ten factors, provides access to the organizational change success diagnostic, and alerts the reader to likely barriers to change. The resultant implementation process can be used by leaders of varying experience to create change in organizations of different size, operating in different industries and market sectors.

Most organization leaders today create change using a trial-and-error process, learning as they go, but at a significant financial and human cost. The impact of trial and error on the performance of the organization, the confidence of the employees within that organization, and the slow speed of change is a negative one that can cause stagnation over many years for the organization and its people. The Mindshop organizational change success model has been used over the last five years at the time of writing this book by thousands of leaders with great success.

The application of the Mindshop organizational change model is both simple and practical. A leader can develop a change initiative plan-which could be the growth of the business, leadership development initiative, or a new product innovation-assess its probability using the Mindshop organizational change diagnostic, identify gaps in the ten factors of the model, develop specific strategies and actions to bridge these gaps, integrate the strategies and actions into the master plan, and seek to lift the probability to 80 percent or higher for success in the implementation of the organizational change initiative.

Organizational Change Research Process (Optional Reading)

There is nothing permanent except change.

— *Heraclitus*

The general problem addressed by this study was that leaders of organizations lacked the guidance of a model that they could use with confidence to implement change successfully. This lack of guidance resulted in significant waste, even the demise of organizations, and a lack of predictability of organizational performance. Researchers found that 70 percent of change initiatives were unsuccessful. The causes of this high failure rate have been identified as factors such as the increased complexity of organizations, resistance to change, lack of valence (the intrinsic attractiveness or goodness or adverseness of an event, object, or situation), leadership style, lack of leader experience, and a lack of change readiness.

The cost of these failures is high and negatively impacts negatively society. The studies of change management have focused on the reasons for failure and not on the development of a new model. Change is critical to the success of an organization. There is a lack of a systematic view and a need for a predictive theory to address this problem. The purpose of the sequential explanatory mixed methods study used for this research was to develop a theory of change success that enabled leaders of organizations to significantly increase the probability of success of their change initiatives. They would be able to do this by the application of specific actions aimed at increasing the change readiness and the change intentions of their people.

Structural equation modelling was used to define the relationship between the variables and to guide the second part of the grounded theory process about participant selection and interview questions. Change management exemplars were interviewed in the second strand, which provided the ability to triangulate the data from both parts of the study and to elaborate on what the key success factors are and how best to implement them. There were 219 leaders and 21 change agents in the first part of the study; for CEOs in the second part, there were 3 leaders and 6 change agents. The CEOs and leaders were recruited from nine organizations (three in Australia, three in the United States, and three in the United Kingdom). The three variables in the study were change success, change readiness, and change intentions.

The four research questions were as follows:

1. What relationship, if any, is there between change intentions and organizational change success for leaders of organizations?
2. What relationship, if any, is there between organizational change readiness and organizational change success for leaders of organizations?
3. How do the variables of change intentions and change readiness predict change success in organizations?
4. What makes some leaders of organizations more successful in implementing a change initiative than other leaders?

The sequential explanatory mixed methodology had the advantage that the quantitative data and results provided a general picture of the research problem and the qualitative data results refined and explained the specific details of the change phenomenon. For example, change readiness was confirmed to have a positive relationship with change success in the grounded theory process that was used to explain how that relationship plays out in the field.

The instruments used in the first qualitative part of the study were in common use, but permission was needed to apply them to this study. The permission to use the change readiness instrument was provided by Achilles Armenakis from Auburn University, and permission to use the change success instrument was provided by Tony Inman. A dedicated website was developed to provide participants with easy access to the consent form, the quantitative survey, and general information about the research and the study. All interviews were recorded and transcripts prepared. The transcripts were analyzed and coded on a line-by-line basis to identify the relationship between the variables. A technique known as an exploratory factor analysis was used on the constructs of change readiness, change intentions, and change success. Structural equation modeling was used to measure the relationship between these variables, and a theoretical model was developed from this data.

The resultant model confirmed that change intentions had no relationship with the actual change success measures of profit, growth, return on investment (ROI), etc. It was interesting to find that capability proved to be significant. This capability was in two parts: the capability of the organization and the capability of everyone that works in that organization. The grounded theory process resulted in confirmation of the factors of change success, organizational capability, personal capability, change environment, and change process. The individual importance of each factor was also quantified.

Organizational Change Literature

The only way to make sense out of change is to plunge into it, move with it, and join the dance.

—*Alan Watts*

My research into organizational change continues and I have made it a priority to continuously search academic databases for interesting new developments. I have selected a sample of the papers that have contributed to the knowledge base of organizational change that I think will be of interest to you. A synopsis of each sample paper and its APA citation follows:

Simpkins, L., & Lemyre, L. (2018). Organizational stewardship: Examining a new measure in the stress and well-being framework. *Canadian Journal of Behavioural Science, 50*(3), 144-155. doi: 10.1037/cbs0000104

Organizational processes and dynamics have a significant influence on the well-being of employees. Executives working in organizations that promote the sharing of power, knowledge, and resources built on a foundation of a sense of purpose and a focus on the common good, can create a culture that results in lower stress and higher well-being. There has been a shift in focus from individual attitudes and behaviors to the underlying factors of the work environment.

Leadership has been considered a personal characteristic whereas stewardship functions beyond any specific interpersonal interaction.

Stewardship is an organizational approach that stresses a sense of purpose focused on the common good. This study examined stewardship in the context of organizational stress and well-being. A sample of 2314 senior executives from the Canadian public service were surveyed to assess the level of stewardship. It was found that stewardship contributed incremental improvement in the relationship between psychological stress and measures of distress, cynicism, and work engagement. Stewardship is considered a significant organizational resource for all leaders.

The stewardship measures developed for this study can be used as a diagnostic tool to help leaders identify training needs or required interventions to offset stressful situations and to build the resilience of employees. If low stewardship is identified the leaders can develop and strengthen stewardship through more purpose focused work practices and procedures that will strengthen the trust between employees. By triggering stewardship work engagement levels can be enhanced and distress and cynicism reduced.

Steinmetz, H., Knappstein, M., Ajzen, I., Scmidt, P., & Kabst, R. (2016). How effective our behavior change interventions based on the theory of planned behavior? *Zeitschrift fur Psychologie, 224(3),* 216-233. doi: 10.1027/2151-2604/a000255

The Theory of Planned Behavior (TPB) was developed by one of the researchers of this meta-analysis, Icek Ajzen from the University of Massachusetts. My research into organizational change in 2014 also used TPB to inform some of the change factors in my original hypothesis. The purpose of this 2016 study was to evaluate the effectiveness of TPB interventions on motivation and behavior in a variety of situations.

Theories such as TPB are used to understand and predict behavior but also to guide change interventions. The key determinant of behavior in the TPB model is the intention to perform that behavior. The assumption is that intentions are the best predictor of behavior. TPB has proven to be a useful framework for designing behavior change interventions.

The TPB theory proposes that beliefs provide the basis for attitudes, subjective norms, and perceptions of behavioral control. Intentions are influenced by attitude towards the behavior. TPB can be used as a theoretical framework intervention aimed at changing behavioral, normative, and control beliefs and so motivating performance of the behavior. The benefit is that a successful intervention could increase a person's beliefs about positive outcomes and decreased beliefs about negative outcomes. It should also raise the perception that significant others will approve of the behavior, increased skills or knowledge, and decrease actual barriers to the change.

The importance of TPB is that it allows researchers to specify methods and target variables with a high likelihood of success. One of the limitations of this meta-analysis is that most of the studies relied exclusively on self-reports of behavior.

Commons, M. L. (2017). Four forces that prevent change in organizations: how to become an innovative organization. *Behavioral Development, 23(1)*, 14-21. doi: 10.1037/bdb0000073

Larger organizations, managed from the top down, tend to be more bureaucratic, less innovative, and more resistant to change. The four forces that prevent a larger organization from changing are, behavioral momentum, regression to the mean, inadequate behavioral development stage of addressing issues, and interaction between the first three variables. It is assumed that in larger organizations the chain of command extends from the top to the bottom implying a greater superiority and domination of the lower levels. In a rapidly changing business environment these characteristics are in fact the death-knell to business success. A highly autonomous two or three-layer flat management structure encourages creativity and innovation. This results in a broad base of leaders and employees who feel a sense of ownership of the overall success of the organization.

The behavioral momentum in larger organizations ensure that orders come from the top and cascade their way down through the various layers of management. This bureaucracy exists to protect against errors. These control-based models have two consequences, too little positive recognition given when things are done well and punitive action swiftly taken when errors are made. This results in employees feeling some resentment towards the company and a failure to adopt an orientation that can contribute to the success of the organization. Leaders do not often seek feedback from their employees resulting in a high level of difficulty in creating change environment. Behavioral momentum can be described as follows: when a response has been reinforced in a distinctive stimulus situation, its rate of occurrence or response rate depends on the response-reinforcer contingencies. The large number of memes found in larger organizations are created by a form of infection. They are the idea and behavior patterns that are common in the day-to-day operations and long-term functioning of the company.

Regression to the mean refers to a phenomenon where even if a variable is extreme on its first measurement, it will eventually move closer to the mean over time. This phenomenon extends to the total memes in an organization insuring that even if an organization overcomes behavioral momentum and adopts a new meme, the meme is always at risk of being lost through influence from the overall culture. This makes it difficult for new and innovative management interventions to have a lasting impact. Often leaders who introduce such memes get fired or retire because of the resistance to change due to the behavioral momentum. Even if the leader is not fired, their ideas are often disregarded, and the company regresses to the mean of the memes.

The solution is to ensure that organizations are smaller and have a flat management structure. Another way of counteracting regression to the mean is through a significant investment in R&D. New and emerging technology can assist with this change process. Acquisition of smaller but more disruptive companies can introduce new memes into the host organization. Risk taking leaders can also be a successful change initiative. Matching the level of the leader with authority is another key success factor. There is little point in hiring a high performing person if he or she does not have the authority to make changes.

Organizational Change Success Model

If you change the way you look at things, the things you look at change.

— WAYNE DYER

THE THREE KEY FACTORS OF organizational change success are change readiness, capability, and the beliefs of the members of the organization. Change readiness is a measure of how ready the organization and the people within the organization are to implement change. Capability is a measure of the skills, people, training, and resources that are needed to implement the change. Beliefs is a summary of the overall attitude of the organization in relation to the specific change. After determining what the key factors were, the next step was to estimate what impact each of these factors had on the overall probability of change success as not all the factors have an equal impact. It was determined that change readiness was 30 percent, beliefs was 30 percent, and capability was 40 percent of the impact of change success.

Change readiness is made up of five individual elements: leadership support, the need for change, what's in it for me (WIIFM), the change process used, and the level of confidence. Capability has two components: people capability and organizational capability. Beliefs has three elements, which are perceived difficulty, attitude, and the impact of significant others. Each of these ten factors is explained in detail in the following chapters.

If you think about your own experience with organizational change, the ten organizational change success factors make sense. Once you see the list, the reaction is normally "I knew that!" When I drafted the hypothesis for my organizational change success research, I did have different expectations for what the resultant ten factors would be. I hadn't thought of capability as a major factor, I had underestimated how important the WIIFM would be, and the change readiness emphasis was more detailed than I could have developed using just common sense and intuition.

The research that established that the normal change success probability is 30 percent did resonate with me. It made me feel guilty about how ineffective I had been in the past. I now understood why it took so much hard work to initially create the change and even more to maintain it.

The organizational change model is shown below:

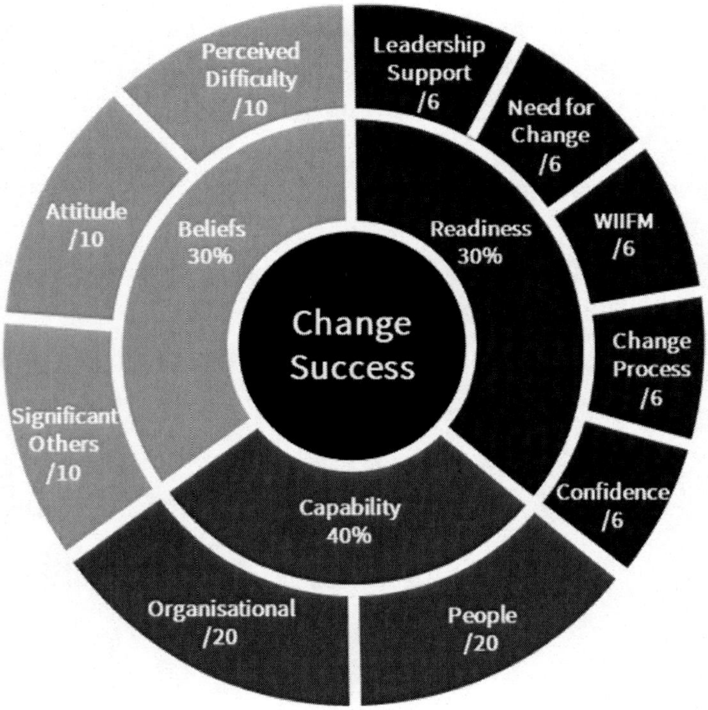

The weight given to each of the ten factors made sense. The fact that capability contributed 40 percent of the probability for an organizational change initiative success, even though I hadn't originally thought of it, felt right. With some rounding for simplification in the field, beliefs and readiness being 30 percent each also felt right. I tested the scoring template against some recent change initiative where I was successful, and the results were close to a 50 percent probability of success. I had some work to do to boost it to 80 percent probability to ensure I maximized my probability of success. I was excited to see how the model could help me.

Organizational Change Success Factor 1—Leadership Support

Change is the law of life. And those who look only to the past or present are certain to miss the future.

—John F. Kennedy

The question is, to what degree does the leader of the change initiative visibly (and emotionally) support the change initiative? It is not uncommon in larger organizations that project teams are established, and the team members have little or no understanding of why the project they are undertaking is so important. In smaller organizations, the team process is less structured; change is implemented as a part of the normal business operations. For all organizations, regardless of size, the change initiative will have a higher probability of success if the team process is more structured.

The organization's leaders need to provide an insightful project brief that clearly defines the importance of the project to the organization, the desired outcomes, and the resources and support the team will be given to enable them to complete its task. Typically, people are expected to participate in a project team and no consideration is given to how the team activities will be managed in terms of cost and time.

The selection of the team leader is one of the key success factors of any project team. It is not recommended that the team be left to decide who will lead it. The team leader should be selected based on capability, ability to lead and motivate the team, perseverance, and respect. Team leaders who prove to be unsuitable need to be replaced. Any failure in the team will reflect badly on the culture of the organization. Team leaders need to clearly understand that they have the full backing of senior management. A team sponsor from the senior management team should be appointed to make sure that any barriers that the team leader experiences can be resolved quickly.

Leaders need to constantly reinforce high levels of direct and indirect support. This can be done through developing the project brief initially, expressing the importance of the project to the team and the organization, and continuously providing the senior management team with progress. With a project team that I set up in the Victorian Police many years ago, we decided to appoint a high-potential but low-level policeman to be the team leader. One of the team members was the regional commander. We made it very clear that rank has no privileges in a project team! The regional commander was there to provide support and context to the project team. While his membership of the team may have constrained some of the open communication, it did enable a rapid and impressive outcome for the team. The project that was undertaken was to improve the utilization of police vehicles; the project took weeks—not months—to complete successfully.

Responsibility for ensuring leadership support to the project team should be shared jointly by the senior management and the team leader. If the team leader perceives there needs to be a higher profile on the team within the organization, then he or she should ask for it. Often senior management assumes that its support of and participation in the change process can be counterproductive to the independence of the team. The opposite is the case. As long as they don't interfere, the more involvement, the better!

Organizational Change Success Factor 2—Need for Change

Change will not come if we wait for some other person or some other time. We are the ones we've been waiting for. We are the change that we seek.

— *Barack Obama*

For this factor the question to ask is, to what degree do the change participants believe that there is a quantifiable need for improvement between the *now* and the *where* with regard to the change initiative? One of the limiting factors in a change initiative is that senior management and the team members can have different views about how important the designated project or change initiative is. Making sure that each of the project team members understands the need for change is a key success factor.

Too often senior management assumes that the lower levels of the organization believe in the need for a factor such as growth. To the senior management, growth represents opportunity, profitability, competitive advantage, and success recognition. To others in the organization, it may represent, potential capacity issues, increased workload, more stress, customer dissatisfaction, and a negative impact on life balance. Team members should be selected partly based on their belief in the importance of the project outcome.

To maximize the impact of this factor leaders need to make sure that in the project brief the need for the outcome targeted by the project team is clearly explained and justified. A second factor would be to reinforce continuously throughout the life of the project the benefits that will be achieved by a successful outcome. The understanding of the need for change needs to be developed into distinct phases. The first phase is to ensure that the need for change is understood by the team leader of the change initiative and his or her team. Unless the team believes there is an important need for change, its investment of time and energy into the team process will be constrained. The second phase is even more important—how the team convinces all other stakeholders in that need to change.

In the project team cycle, which I will cover in detail later in this book, the team reaches a point at which it needs to determine how it will implement its change initiative. It is at this point that team members need to consider how they will communicate to the rest the organization, particularly key stakeholders, the importance and need for their solution and recommendations. It is common that the team is not going to be the one responsible for implementing the outcomes of its work. If it's a new methodology for improving profitability, for example, then it is likely that every employee will have a role in achieving that goal. The challenge for the project team then becomes what will it need to recommend so that people believe in the need for increased profitability. Obviously, leadership support will be one key factor, but there will be others. Another will be showing all employees what the personal benefit to them will be; we call that the what's in it for me.

Organizational Change Success Factor 3—WIIFM

When we are no longer able to change a situation,
we are challenged to change ourselves.

— *Victor E. Frankl*

For this factor, the question is, to what degree do the change participants see the benefit for themselves in participating in the change initiative? Research has found that the higher the personal benefit, the what's in it for me (WIIFM), the higher the impact it will have on the organizational change potential score. Examples of these benefits include specialist training, higher organizational profile, and leadership experience. Leaders cannot assume that the team members, or indeed the organization, will accept that the change will be beneficial. There is a common belief that people don't like change; it is my belief that is more likely to be that they do not appreciate the change because its benefit has not been adequately explained.

There are both short-term and long-term benefits to be gained through participating in or leading a change initiative. Increased profile within the organization, increased skills, enhanced career prospects, and personal growth are just some of the benefits. I often suggest to senior management that the project leader is someone who would benefit from all these benefits, as well as from receiving coaching from a person like me. Often team members are more concerned about the costs of participation than the benefits. They worry about workload, their ability to deliver what is required, and being linked with a potential project failure! A good question to ask a potential team leader is, "What do you need to 100 percent guarantee the success of this project?"

Do not assume what the benefit to an individual will be. You need to ask them what they think they will get from it. It is not only things that benefit them personally. It is often things like improved customer service, more sales, higher efficiency, or even job satisfaction from the rest of the team. Some people think like an owner; it is wrong to assume they don't!

The constraint is often around the issue of trust. Can they trust you to support them? Can they trust you to reward them? Can they trust themselves to be committed to the project? Can they trust you when you say that the project is only for eight weeks? If you identify any of these lack of trust issues, then you need to build into the project brief fixes for them. A way of filtering out people who have a trust issue is to use volunteers to staff your project teams. The only downside that you need to be aware of in this case is to make sure that the people volunteering have the required capability to contribute to the project.

A good test of the WIIFM is whether you would volunteer to be part of the team. Your involvement does not need to be on a full-time basis. You could be a subject matter expert that they could bring in on an as-needed basis. What would be the WIIFM for you in this case? For me, it would be things like knowledge transfer, value to others, effective use of my time, and a bit of fun. As a leader, you need to be willing to do whatever you're asking others to do, but it doesn't mean that you need to; it's just a good test to apply before asking for volunteers. The fact that you are asking them for a limited investment of time will make it easier for them to accept your offer.

If you are following the Mindshop change initiative process, then the duration of the team should be limited to around eight weeks.

People will volunteer for an eight-week project; it is not likely they will volunteer when the time expectation is either unspecified or unknown. So what will be the process that we will use over the eight-week life of the change initiative?

Organizational Change Success Factor 4—Change Process

Just when I think I have learned the way to live, life changes.

— Hugh Prather

One issue that is not often considered is to what degree do the change participants believe that the change process being used is the most appropriate for the change initiative. If we are using a trial-and-error approach with the normal 30 percent probability of success, then it will lower the confidence people have in the change process we will be using. Mindshop is a well-proven process for change and one based on evidence. At best, most organizations have a hybrid process where they use a combination of experience, ideas from conferences and books, and whatever the leader has as the current flavor of the month by way of a model or concept. This does not give confidence to the organization that we have chosen the best possible change process for the specific outcome we need to achieve. Most are too rigid or complex to work in the fast-paced business environment we all operate in.

The ideal change process is one that has been used with success within the organization over a long period of time. If that experience is not present, then the next best option is to pick a change process that has been used with success within other organizations over a long period of time. The people involved in the change initiative need to feel confident that the methodology chosen will work in their industry and for their size of organization. Too much adaptation can produce uncertainty and distrust in the change process. A trusted peer can often suggest processes and resources that they have found to work well.

The key success factors of the Mindshop change process are the following:

- an evidence-based change model with a proven 80 percent probability of success
- best practice tools and processes for problem-solving, project team implementation, KPIs, and coaching resources
- an online support platform that provides a 24/7 self-help resource so that team leaders can be confident that they have both the support and best practice tools to ensure their success
- thousands of successful applications of the change process over many countries and a variety of industries and organization sizes

There are other change processes available in the market; they can be tested against the four characteristics of the Mindshop process listed above. If you find that another process is better, use it (and let me know why you thought it was better so that we can continuously improve the Mindshop process)! People involved in the change initiative need to be confident that the most appropriate change process will be used to achieve their project goals. The next challenge is to decide how this is best accomplished.

Organizational Change Success Factor 5—Confidence

Some people don't like change, but you need to embrace change if the alternative is disaster.

— *Elon Musk*

Confidence has two key elements to consider. Participants in the change process need to be confident that the organization will do what it says about elements such as support, the duration of the project, the importance of the project, and the personal benefits that will be achieved through the successful completion of the project. If in the past there have been situations where senior management has not provided support or resources for a change initiative, then this will impact negatively on the current participants' confidence in the leadership support for the proposed change initiative. History can become a negative factor when someone in the organization makes comments like, "We tried that in the past and it didn't work!" When I hear comments like this, my standard response is, "So what were the lessons from the failure in the past? What can we learn, what can we change, what do we need to do to 100 percent guarantee a successful outcome this time?"

The second element of confidence is related to the organizational confidence, but it is more about the personal confidence of the change initiative participants. If people believe that they do not have everything required to be successful, they will not be confident about being part of the process. They may perceive that they do not have the relevant experience, training, influence, and approvals required for success. This perception may even be partly correct. They may be missing some key elements. This is where the benefit of team selection kicks in. It is unlikely that any individual has everything required for the team's success. It is vital that every need is met by someone, even if they are not a full-time member of the change initiative team. Remember what I said about subject matter experts. In setting up the project team, we need to consider all the requirements, but if we overlook any, there is nothing to stop us from bringing in whatever experience or skill is missing from the original team. The importing of these special requirements can be done on a full-time or part-time basis, depending on what it is. Our willingness to do this needs to be stressed at the time of the team formation. This heads off any concerns around confidence.

A good tactic is to make a list of all the strengths of each person in the team, as well as any subject matter experts or sponsors that will be used to support the team. When this list is reviewed by the team members, it should reinforce that we have sufficient talent and expertise to do the job. When developing such a list, do not ignore some of the soft resource requirements, such as leadership, motivation, resilience, and determination. These team requirements are as important as the hard skills and experience, such as financial, engineering, legal, sales, quality, research, and operations.

If you need to develop the confidence levels of the people involved in a change initiative, one way to achieve this is to engineer their success, at least in the early stages. Breaking a project into stages that have an ever-increasing level of difficulty enables people to gain experience and build confidence in a low-risk setting. Working in a group, regardless of size, enables a transfer of knowledge and skill between one group member to another. The leverage that comes from working with others can be significant.

You could expect that throughout the duration of the team cycle, there will be significant knowledge gained by every participant. The skill transfer that comes from working together, the need to learn new things, and the experience gained from the successful implementation of the project team add to the experience of everyone and have a positive impact on self-confidence. One of the risks will be whether we have all the capability that we need for the change initiative project team to be successful.

Organizational Change Success Factor 6—People Capability

Money and success don't change people; they merely amplify what is already there.

— Will Smith

PEOPLE CAPABILITY (EQUAL TO ORGANIZATIONAL capability) is one of the highest impact factors of the change success model. The question to ask in this case is, to what degree do the change participants believe that they have the capability to perform in a reliable and satisfactory way the tasks required by the change initiative? Keep in mind that there are two dimensions to capability: operational (capabilities that are required to earn a living) and dynamic (capabilities that enable you to improve how you earn a living).

The operational capabilities normally include things like time management, delegation, self-motivation, and technical skills. The dynamic capabilities include learning, innovation, use of technology, and personal networks. There are several factors that positively impact both operational and dynamic capabilities including, communication, public speaking, strategic planning, and self-confidence. In total, to build capability requires training, knowledge, and experience in all these factors.

Team selection can have a large impact on the people capability being applied to the project. I have experienced situations where people have been appointed to a team because they either had the time to do it or needed to improve their performance. Neither of these characteristics can be considered operational or dynamic capabilities. Often our most talented people are fully occupied and do not readily have time available to invest in a project team. Change fatigue is a common problem in most organizations globally. The responsibility for managing change in any size organization often falls to the most capable (because they are trusted and reliable), and the additional duties associated with the change initiative are added to an existing full workload.

This is where you can apply the Pareto rule to overcome the change fatigue. With anyone, even our most talented people, 20 percent of their activity generates 80 percent of the value that they are to the organization. It is in the 80 percent of the low-value activities that we can find time for participation in a project team. Time can be created by either delegation to others or just stopping (even if just for the short term) some specific activities. This does not mean that every team member in the change initiative team needs to be one of the most talented employees. The team leader certainly needs to be drawn from that pool, but high-potential people can also be selected. A strategically important change initiative project team can often be a good experience for these high-potential people, and it will provide an opportunity to build relationships with some of the current and future leaders of the organization.

You may want to offer coaching support to the team leader to enhance his or her leadership capability. This just-in-time learning in which the coaching is applied directly to a short-term problem or opportunity is usually the most effective way of teaching key skills. As I keep stating, training courses, books, and even formal education are just the tickets to the game; the real learning occurs when this newly gained knowledge is applied in the real world. The people capability is not just a factor for how the project team will work, it is also a consideration that the team needs to reflect on when they develop their recommendations for implementation—will the organization itself be capable?

Organizational Change Success Factor 7—Organizational Capability

Change before you have to.

—*Jack Welch*

LIKE PERSONAL CAPABILITY, ORGANIZATIONAL CAPABILITY has the same two dimensions of operational capability and dynamic capability. In this case, operational capabilities are those required for the organization to operate successfully, and dynamic capabilities are those that enable the improvement of the success of the organization. Organizational capabilities of all types are normally applicable to most activities within the organization.

Operational capability will cover the aspects of marketing, sales, operations, performance management, finance, and customer service. It is the dynamic capabilities that create the success of the organization. These aspects include product innovation, growth strategies, attraction and retention of good employees, and culture development. If the organization is good at most things, then it is likely that aspects such as leadership, project management, accountability, and employee engagement are also good. Unfortunately, the converse is also true. A change initiative project team's success is directly linked to these aspects.

It is likely that the change initiative project team will make some assumptions regarding the organizational capability with variables such as communication, funding, staffing, and leadership. The effectiveness of any of the team recommendations will be constrained by failures in areas such as these. It is not uncommon to run into an organizational change barrier that becomes insurmountable and indirectly conflicts with the recommendations of the change initiative team. I remember one such situation where the project team was trying to solve the issue of growth and recommended that some new value-added services be integrated into the product offering. To have the capability required to provide such services needed the recruitment of some new people to the organization with those skills. The roadblock that the organization inadvertently had in place was a belief of senior management that no new employees could be employed without proof that the existing sales were in place. Common sense should have dictated that the sales were not possible without the new people, but the belief and practice of not employing people until the demand was there was even stronger. The proposed initiative failed!

The project team, if they had thought more deeply about the organizational capability, could have suggested that a strategic alliance with a third-party specialist in the value-added services area be established, revenue generated, and internal resources gradually be recruited in reaction to the increased revenue demand. This solution would have been the obvious one if the organizational capability roadblock had been considered at the recommendation stage.

Perhaps if the project team had been advised by a team sponsor from the senior management team, they would have identified the blockage. This reinforces that we need to take into consideration the likely reaction of the key people within the organization when framing our strategies and actions.

Organizational Change Success Factor 8—Significant Others

Things don't have to change the world to be important.

— Steve Jobs

The term *significant others*, in the context of a change initiative, refers to the people significant to the team member of the change initiative; the relationship could be professional or personal. The question for this factor is, to what degree do the change participants believe that the people significant to them think their participation in the change initiative is important? There is often an assumption that the significant others to an employee would include their leaders. Research has found that this is not always the case; in fact, peers and close family members are often more significant than leaders.

If we assume that the average person has ten significant others in their life, it may be that in the context of a change initiative project team, only five of these are relevant. The challenge is to identify who these five people are and make sure they understand the significance and relevance of the change initiative. The project team member needs to believe that these five significant others support the initiative. This may require a firmwide communication plan to ensure everyone, including the significant others, understands what is about to happen and why.

Having identified the significant others relevant to the organization and the team members of the specific change initiative, it is essential that you work out how best to engage them. An obvious way is to invite them to be either part of the project team, a subject matter expert available to that team, or even the sponsor. Often cross-functional teams take on projects that have a significant impact on a department within the organization. One example I experienced was a team charged with developing a sales process for the organization. The head of business development was a significant other and to ensure support for the project this individual was invited to help produce the project brief. It was stressed from that point on that the project team needed to ensure that the head of business development would be able to approve the recommendations made by the project team. The project team needed this significant other to sign off on the report before it could be presented to senior management. Anticipating concerns of significant others is a key factor in the success of any change initiative.

Make a list of the significant others and check it for accuracy from a variety of vantage points. One obvious vantage point would be from the perception of senior management. Another would be asking people in the operational areas of the business who they think would be the most knowledgeable on the change initiative topic. Often names you would not automatically consider get revealed in this way. Do not be surprised to find that the list from senior management has significant differences to the list gained by speaking to people on the shop floor of the organization. The key element that differentiates a significant other from everyone else in the organization is their attitude to the proposed change initiative.

Organizational Change Success Factor 9—Attitude

All changes, even the most longed for, have their melancholy; for what we leave behind us is a part of ourselves; we must die to one life before we can enter another.

— *Anatole France*

You cannot assume what the attitude of stakeholders will be towards a specific change initiative. There are many factors that will impact attitude. People who have worked in the organization for a long time may have the attitude that things are fine as they are, the current procedures are well proven over a long time, and any change puts the success of the organization at risk. Other people may see it differently. Maybe they see it as an opportunity for change. They may have recently joined the organization and have relevant experience on the topic from the perspective of their previous employment.

A good example is one from a professional service firm where one of the partners of the firm had recently returned from maternity leave. We will call her Joan (not her real name). At a partner meeting, all partners were told that they needed to increase sales significantly as several key clients had been lost over the previous year. The managing partner asked everyone at the meeting to confirm that they were fully behind this initiative. Everyone agreed regardless of their attitude. They knew it would be a career limiting move if they were seen to have any different views about this proposed growth.

As Joan left the room she thought, "I agree that we need more revenue, but I'm not coping now trying to balance my family and work responsibilities. Last time I asked for help I didn't get any. If I win all this work, who will do it?" The conflicts in Joan's attitude toward sales growth are likely to lead to her not achieving the goal set by her managing partner. All the managing partner will see is Joan's failure if the attitudes that have impacted this result are not anticipated.

One way to counteract this problem would be to propose the objective of sales growth but then identify the likely barriers to growth. Issues, such as capacity, capability, delegation, attraction and retention of good staff, may then get identified and form part of the growth plan. Too often leaders specify outcomes that they desire without considering how such a result can be achieved. Anticipation of the attitudes of stakeholders and the change initiative team members must be undertaken to develop a robust plan.

Closely associated with attitude is the factor of perceived difficulty. Most of us have an aversion to failure. We can increase the probability of success by taking on less difficult tasks. How much waste then occurs due to our perception of the degree of difficulty of a challenge or opportunity we are facing? How could we reduce this waste?

Organizational Change Success Factor 10—Perceived Difficulty

In order to change the world, you have to get your head together first.

—Jimi Hendrix

THE FINAL ORGANIZATIONAL CHANGE FACTOR is the perceived difficulty in achieving the desired goal. This factor is linked to several of the other change success factors for organizational change but the question that needs to be asked is, to what degree do the change participants feel that they have everything they need to be able to achieve the required tasks? If they feel they are not well resourced, have the skills and knowledge required, that the objective for the change initiative is realistic and achievable, then it will negatively impact their likely success. If it is perceived to be too difficult because of these factors, then the probability of success lowers.

One of the subtle factors impacting perceived difficulty is the amount of time they can invest in the change initiative. When people perceive that they are already busy, they may think that they will not have any additional time to work on a project team. This is where I normally remind them of the Pareto rule. In this context, the Pareto rule suggests that 20 percent of what they are currently doing is creating 80 percent of the benefit they are to their organization. This means that the other 80 percent of what they do has a significantly reduced impact. By identifying what activities are in this area, time can be created to work on the change initiative.

Related to the concerns around time is the concern around duration. If you ask someone to work on a project team for an indefinite period, the degree of difficulty is considered much higher than if you ask them to work on the project team for just an eight-week period. That is why I recommend eight-week team cycles for any size project. The challenge then is to make sure that the project scope is such that the problem or opportunity can be resolved within that period.

It is common to set an eight-week project on a larger issue, and one of the recommendations from the project team is to do further work using other project teams. My view is that you make more money when you work *on* the business than you do when you work *in* the business. Working on the business implies strategy, problem-solving, business improvement, process improvement, quality, customer service, and profitability. Why put more business through an incapable system? I consider it significantly better use of my time to work out how I can work on the system capability rather than just trying to improve the throughput on the current system. When people understand this philosophy and are working in a team, their perception of the degree of difficulty decreases. Another benefit is that their motivation increases.

An obvious way of reducing the perception of difficulty in a change initiative is to enlist the support of subject matter experts in the area of focus within the change initiative team. The key advantage of taking this approach is the knowledge transfer that normally occurs during the process. If you are a change agent who has considerable experience in guiding change initiative teams, then your involvement can reduce the concerns that the project is too difficult. If you are a leader in your organization and want that same benefit, you could hire a change agent to assist you in bridging the gap on perceived difficulty. Over time, you will develop the same level of experience, confidence, and expertise as the change agent. If you can do this, then change will become a normal part of your leadership activities. You will be working on the business more than you work in it. This is a sign of exceptional leadership and should be the goal of anyone in such a role in an organization or in their community.

Case Study—Organizational Change Success

Change means that what was before wasn't perfect. People want things to be better.

— *Esther Dyson*

UNDERSTANDING AND IMPLEMENTING THE TEN change success factors for a change initiative in an organization in theory allows you to lift your probability of success from 30 percent to 80 percent Learning these factors is just the ticket to the game; the real learning occurs when you apply this knowledge. A pilot project is often a safe environment to practice the change process. I recommend that you keep it small and manageable to reduce any risk of failure. Ultimately, you should consider doing this on your own organization, but I would like to share one of my change projects with you to demonstrate how the process is applied. The context I am using is that you are an adviser to the organization rather than a leader because that was my role in the case study. If you were the leader, much of the process would remain the same.

The case study is a professional service firm that I will call ABC LLP. The firm is based in the Midwest of the United States, a medium-sized accounting firm with 15 partners. The clients of the firm are diversified and work in industries such as retail, manufacturing, banking, and technology. The revenue of the firm is split between one-third from tax compliance, one-third from audit services, and the remaining third from value-added services. The managing partner of the firm operates as a benevolent dictatorship where most decisions are influenced by him.

As the founding partners started to consider retirement, it became obvious that there was a significant gap in leadership capability between them and the rest of the organization. The culture of the organization was all about short-term fees rather than leveraging the clients through growing the value-added services. The reliance solely on compliance services over time became more difficult, in part due to the continued commoditization of tax and audit. The aging partners either consciously or subconsciously accepted this change but were unwilling to invest for the future due to their pending exit from the firm. This meant that many capable and high-potential accountants got frustrated and left the organization. The stoic senior staff hung in, in the hope that they would be promoted once the founders exited.

Unfortunately, the exit was delayed, and when it did happen after an extended period of little or no change, the accounting firm had been significantly disrupted. As new leaders emerged from within the ranks of the remaining staff, they were faced with a difficult road to rebuild the firm. So how can these new leaders ensure that they will be successful? Mindshop has a series of diagnostics that were used to identify the key issues and the current probability of success of any future change initiatives. The Mindshop GPS diagnostic identified the following factors as being relevant. Three areas of weakness were identified as leadership, strategy, and people. The three areas of strength were systems, technology, and implementation. The Mindshop organizational change success diagnostic reported that capability was the biggest challenge, specifically organizational capability. The change readiness was relatively low because of poor scores in leadership support, confidence, and a lack of understanding of the what's in it for me (WIIFM). In the need for change, one of the readiness factors was high but the other four readiness factors scored poorly. On the belief component of the change success model, the three areas of perceived difficulty, attitude, and significant others also scored low. The total score for probability of success came in at 48 percent. This meant that the firm only had a fifty-fifty chance of succeeding; the challenge then was how do we get that to 80 percent?

A plan was developed driven by an understanding of the sustainable competitive advantage (SCA), which then helped identify the key issues as growth, profit, and engagement. A strategic strengths, weaknesses, opportunities, and threats (SWOT) analysis was undertaken to develop the strategies and action plans required. With the plan drafted, it was then tested against the ten organizational change success factors. A brief overview of how each of the factors was used to achieve an 80 percent probability of success follows:

1. **Leadership support**. The key leaders were directly involved in the project team implementation process. Reports at partner meetings reinforced the importance of the change activities. Successes were celebrated. People were rewarded and recognized for their contributions.
2. **Need for change**. The management team explained clearly why change was required. Change was seen to be a high priority because the ways of old were no longer working. This message was continuously reinforced.
3. **WIIFM**. Considerable thought was given to how to benefit those participating in the change process. Recognition, learning opportunities, even promotion, were used to provide benefit. It was decided to grow talent in-house rather than import it.
4. **Change process**. The Mindshop tools and processes were the foundation for each change initiative. Several licensed Mindshop facilitators were already in place in the firm, and they were used to support project teams and maintain the strategy.
5. **Confidence**. My role as a coach and strategist was used to reinforce the confidence of the senior management team. I was

not visible to most employees but heavily involved behind-the-scenes. Over time, I was able to wind back the intensity of my involvement.

6. **People capability**. Even though there was some formal training provided, the real learning came through the change process itself.
7. **Organizational capability**. With many of the change blockers now gone, it became much easier to improve processes and performance.
8. **Significant others**. There were five or six key people all fully engaged and committed to the long-term success of the firm. Their commitment was not assumed, but it did need to be managed. I am sure many of the key people thought about other options as we moved through the change process but, thankfully, all are still in place today.
9. **Attitude**. Maybe we were lucky, but only a few good people left. Some people found the increased pressure on accountability not to their liking and left of their own accord. This distillation of attitude resulted in a strong people position within the firm.
10. **Perceived difficulty**. The stress and workload at the start was significant. Over time, as people learned new skills and found new levels of confidence, the day-to-day activities became much easier. The perception of difficulty reduced, and optimism return to the organization.

Hopefully you have the perception that this business has turned around. On reflection about the key success factors, and admitting my own bias, I would think the issues of removing the negative people, harnessing the energies of the younger more ambitious people through a structured plan, supporting those people to guarantee the outcome, and then achieving tangible success that reinforced the positive behaviors were the key success factors. As a total package, yes, this was a challenging program, but when you break it into its component parts, each are easy to replicate. The broad steps in the process included the following:

1. Developing an accurate picture of the starting point, the *now*, using the GPS and change success diagnostics
2. Using the sustainable competitive advantage (SCA) to identify the key issues and then establishing project teams over eight-week cycles to implement the change
3. Identifying the gaps in the ten items of the change success model to ensure probability of success increase from 48 percent to 80 percent.
4. Supporting and training the emerging leaders and building their confidence and capability through their involvement in the change process
5. Making sure the outcomes were specific and measurable so that the stakeholders could quantify the rewards from their efforts

I am confident that if you follow these steps and the specific actions described in the case study, you will also be successful. Obviously, every organization is different. The problems and opportunities vary from organization to organization, but the structure and process of the change model has been well proven in the five years since it was developed.

Organizational Change Diagnostics

For changes to be of any true value, they've
got to be lasting and consistent.

— *Tony Robbins*

Having now seen how essential diagnostics are to the change process, I think we need to share the specific details of both the GPS and change success diagnostics with you. Mindshop people can access the diagnostic through a web-based link, and we have provided that for you as well. When you complete a diagnostic, you will be required to enter in an email address so that you can immediately receive a report on what your key issues are. For those not wanting to do this, we have also provided a hardcopy version that you can score manually.

GPS Business Diagnostic

The link to the 25-question online version of the GPS business diagnostic follows: http://www.web.mindshop.com/gpsnew/

Organizational Change Success Diagnostic

The link to the online version of the change success diagnostic follows: https://www.web.mindshop.com/change-success/

You can manually score the ten organizational change success elements to identify any gaps and your current probability of success for implementing a change initiative in the template following. The ten elements are listed under the headings of readiness, capability, and beliefs. The maximum weight for each of the elements is shown; for example, the maximum score for leadership support is 6 percent. All you need to do is to score each of the ten elements and total the scores for readiness, capability, and beliefs. Ensure you are realistic in your scoring. The total score for all three factors will give you your current probability of success for the organizational change initiative that you have in mind. It is not uncommon to find that your score for the current situation is in the range of 30 percent to 50 percent. Your challenge is to get the total score to at least 80 percent. Look at the areas of biggest gaps in your ten elements. What strategies and actions can you put in place to bridge those gaps? These strategies and actions need to be added to your organizational change initiative plan to boost the probability of a successful implementation to at least 80 percent.

	Factors	Now	Where	Gap	Strategy
READINESS 30%	Leadership Support		6		
	Need for Change		6		
	What's in it for me		6		
	Change Process		6		
	Confidence		6		
	Total		30		
CAPABILITY 40%	People		20		
	Organisational		20		
	Total		40		
BELIEFS 30%	Significant Others		10		
	Attitude		10		
	Perceived Difficulty		10		
	Total		30		
	Total		100		

Organizational Change Beliefs

If you want to change attitudes, start with change in behavior.

— *William Glasser*

Having identified the issues and opportunities in your organization and on the verge of covering how to implement the change process, we need to double-check that we have not inadvertently been influenced by any of biases. The following list of commonly accepted biases is worth reviewing to see if any resonate with you. You could use it as a checklist to determine whether you or any other person involved in your change initiative is subject to any biases. It is a comprehensive list, and some of the biases flow into personal change. I have listed some more biases in the personal change success section of the book.

Ambiguity effect: This cognitive bias impacts decision-making of individuals because of their perception of a lack of information or even ambiguity with that information. It suggests that people select options for which the probability of a favorable outcome is already known to the detriment of an option where the probability of a favorable outcome is unknown.

Anchoring: This bias occurs when individuals over rely on an initial piece of data they have when making decisions. The anchoring bias occurs during decision-making when the individual relies heavily on an initial piece of information to make further judgements.

Authority bias: When a person attributes greater accuracy to the opinions of a person perceived to be an authority figure in their lives, it is known as authority bias. They tend to be more influenced by the opinions of the authority figure.

Bandwagon effect: As more people start believing in something, others tend to hop on the bandwagon inspired by any underlying evidence. This is known as the bandwagon effect and produces a tendency to follow the beliefs and actions of others because of a need to conform and fit in.

Belief bias: A person is more likely to accept an argument that supports an outcome closely aligned to that person's prior experiences, values, and beliefs. There is a tendency to reject any counterarguments that oppose their existing beliefs. Belief bias is a very common and significant form of error.

Confirmation bias: A person is subject to cognitive bias when the individual selectively gathers or recalls information and then interprets it in a biased way. Confirmation bias is more likely to occur when dealing with emotionally charged issues or long-held beliefs.

Courtesy bias: This is the tendency that some people have of not fully revealing their unhappiness or dissatisfaction with a service or product. This occurs because of their desire to not offend the person or organization they are relating to.

Framing effect: When people decide on options based on how well they are framed, they perceive that they are more likely to avoid risk when a positive frame is presented. Some people have a tendency to see situations as a glass half empty, whereas others see them as half full.

Halo effect: When someone assumes additional or even ambiguous information during an initial assessment of another person or situation, they are being impacted by the halo effect. The halo effect can be triggered by the discovery of a common interest, like a football team, a school they attended, or even where they live.

Illusion of control: People often tend to overestimate their ability to control events in their lives. A common example is when people gamble or when they have a belief in the paranormal. This is often due to a lack of insight into their actual ability to control events. They may see themselves as responsible for events even when there is no causal link. The illusion is stronger in situations that are stressful and competitive, which often occurs in a work environment.

Information bias: When people rely on data that is subject to a measurement error, this is referred to as information bias. The error can be an underestimation or overestimation of the actual data. This often occurs in situations like budgeting, finance, or performance management.

Negativity bias: Also known as the negativity effect, this bias occurs when although things are equal, those of a more negative nature have a greater impact on someone's decision-making than neutral or positive things. Something very positive will generally have less of an impact on a person than something equally emotional but negative.

Not invented here: Some people and organizations avoid using other people's products and services because of their belief that in-house developments are better suited and incur lower cost than using outside products and services. This results in an unwillingness to adopt other ideas and it is a form of tribalism.

Optimism bias: When people believe they are less likely to experience a negative event, it is often called unrealistic optimism. There are four factors that can cause a person to be optimistically biased: the outcome they desire, their cognitive thinking process, the data they have about themselves compared to others, and their overall mood. This can result in people believing that they are less likely to experience a crime or a car accident; even smokers may believe they are less likely to contract lung cancer or another disease. This leads to people taking more risks and not ensuring safety measures and risk mitigation strategies are in place.

Outcome bias: An outcome bias is an error made during the evaluation of the quality of a decision where the outcome of that decision is already known. It is like hindsight bias, but hindsight bias focuses on memory distortion, whereas outcome bias focuses on weighing the past outcome heavier than other data when deciding if a previous decision was correct.

Overconfidence bias: Overconfidence can occur in three ways: overestimation of the person's actual performance, over placement of one's performance compared to others, and over precision in awarding unjustified certainty regarding the accuracy of one's own beliefs.

Shared information bias: When a group of people invest their time and energy discussing information that they all are already familiar with and less time and energy discussing information only known to some of the members, this is termed shared information bias. This can result in poor decision-making because the group does not have access to unshared information. This bias often occurs when there are time pressures to reach a decision quickly.

System justification: When people are more satisfied in their defense and justification of the status quo, they often have a need for order, stability, and a lack of change. This is in part due to a person's desire to hold positive attitudes about themselves, the groups they belong to, and the overall social structure in which they operate. Their justification of the system in which they exist is based on the status quo being seen as good, legitimate, and desirable.

Organizational Barriers to Change

Change the changeable, accept the unchangeable,
and remove yourself from the unacceptable.

— *Denis Waitley*

In addition to the individual biases of the team members, there are barriers to change that need to be anticipated and mitigated when implementing a change initiative. Failure to anticipate change barriers is a common failing of leaders of organizations. With over forty years of experience dealing with such barriers, I believe the challenge is to identify just five that are currently having the biggest impact. The good news is that with anticipation, each can be easily dealt with through good planning.

1. **Capability of the team leader**. This is part of the capability factor of the Mindshop organizational change success model. The selection of the team leader for the change initiative is a critical success factor. The role of the team leader is to provide the structure, discipline, motivation, and innovation that results in an insightful solution to the team's project brief. Even if a very capable team leader is selected, it is highly recommended that a support mechanism is provided to that leader. Coaching by

someone more experienced in change implementation is one part of the support, but access to the required resources needed by the team also needs to be considered. These resources can include things like available time, meeting space, capable team members, and support by senior management.

2. **A clear project brief**. This barrier is impacted by all the readiness elements of the Mindshop organizational change success model. A clear project brief can reinforce leadership support, the need for change, the WIIFM, the change process to be used, and it directly impacts the confidence each employee has in their leaders and in themselves to be successful with the change initiative. The problem that the project team is given to resolve must be defined so that the outcomes to be achieved are specific and measurable. If the project has been established to improve sales in the organization, then sales need to be defined to enable a clear target to be set. The ideal project brief should include information such as definition of outcomes, resources available, project sponsor, team members, time frame, leadership support, likely barriers, and the reason why the project has been selected.
3. **Training**. The training provided to people participating in the change initiative will impact the elements of the Mindshop organizational change success model. Training can assist in developing a good attitude towards the change initiative, reducing any concerns about the perceived difficulty, developing the capability of the people involved, and positively impacting their confidence. Training in problem-solving tools is normally required. It should not be assumed that people have fluency in problem-solving tools, such as mind mapping, Pareto, force field analysis, decision-making, and one-page plans. Access to a coach or trainer in additional problem-solving tools is also highly recommended. Depending on the project scope, there may be additional training or briefing on technical aspects of the project and advanced problem-solving tools. Ideally, the training should

be available online so that the training does not need to be scheduled and is available on a self-serve basis.

4. **Resistance to change**. The elements of the Mindshop organizational change success model relevant to this barrier include the need for change, attitude, and perceived difficulty. Resistance to change can be experienced from people not directly involved with the change initiative process. If the project outcomes are likely to challenge people not directly involved in the project team, then consideration needs to be given to how to keep these people informed regarding the team process and the likely recommendations arising from the project team report. These key people not part of the project team can be considered as subject matter experts and invited to sit in on team meetings. Another alternative is to have the team leader regularly brief these other people. Once the team has determined its recommendations, you need to then review those with the ten organizational change success factors. Factors such as need for change and what's in it for me will help develop an implementation strategy that achieves an 80 percent probability of success despite any resistance to change.
5. **Lack of confidence**. This might seem to be an odd barrier, but it is one that is often found in both the team and in the implementation process. This barrier is a clear fit with the confidence element of the readiness factor in the Mindshop organizational change success model. A lack of confidence in the team may come about from a lack of skill or experience (overcome through training and coaching) or a concern about whether senior management will support the team recommendations (leadership support is required here). One way of testing any missing capability is to ensure that the team recommendations are staged. What this means is that the overall recommendation is staged into four steps. Success at step one must occur before moving to step two and so on. This tests the appetite of the organization to embrace the team's recommended changes.

The five barriers listed will address 90 percent of the likely problems that a project team will encounter. If the team is resourced well, and those resources include a coach trained and experienced in implementing a change initiative, then the probability of success is very high. Once a track record of successful change initiative implementation is established, the confidence of future teams will increase, and your ability to attract people to participate in a change initiative (particularly for a period of only eight weeks) becomes much easier. We need good people and those of high potential to be participating in our change initiative teams. We need to make their participation a key part of their fast-track development plan as future leaders.

When a team finishes their project, there must be a celebration. Even just having senior management attend the team presentation and show enthusiasm for and appreciation of the team's work is a form of celebration. You can have pizzas and beer if you like, but just a simple thank you will be regarded more positively by the team, particularly when they already know they have done a good job. The key then is to make sure you engineer the good job. A project team should not ever fail; if it does, it is because the barriers were not anticipated and mitigated right from the start!

Implementation of an Organizational Change Initiative

The world hates change, yet it is the only thing that has brought progress.

— Charles Kettering

Hopefully you are now more confident of the specific areas requiring change when reflecting on your specific change initiative. We have used diagnostics to identify the contender issues or opportunities requiring change, reviewed our potential biases, and discussed potential barriers to change. All we now need is a clear process to make it all happen. Even though the following steps are generalized, they will work for most organizational change initiatives regardless of whether you are a small, micro business or a large multinational.

Step 1—Define clearly the problem or opportunity. If you do not get this right, you will be potentially solving the wrong issue! Take your time to get a specific and measurable project or initiative to work on. For example, defining the problem as "improve profit" can mean a multitude of things, and it will be hard to define. A problem defined as "improve the profitability of X product in Y market by 25 percent by the end of the current calendar year" is clearer.

Step 2—Measure the start point. Now you will see why it is so essential to define the problem or opportunity as clearly as possible. It is essential that you measure the start point of the change process; otherwise, you will not know if your change initiative has made any difference. In the example provided in step one, we need to measure the current profitability of product X in market Y currently. In fact, it would be helpful if we went back at least five years and looked at how that profit performance has been trending.

Step 3—Audit the current change success potential. Use the organizational change success diagnostic to quantify the current change success score with regard to the change initiative. You will remember that the average probability of success of a change initiative is around 30 percent. Even if your audit reveals that the change success potential is around 50 percent, this means that you only have a fifty-fifty chance of succeeding with your proposed profit improvement change initiative. Review each of the ten scores and determine where the gaps are. Is it leadership support, personal capability, or attitude, or is it one of the other seven organizational change success factors? Having these gaps in mind will help you design the rest of the process. It will also be interesting to see how the score changes over the life of your change initiative.

Step 4— Have a clear project brief. You may have been given a project brief, or you have been asked to develop one. In either case, here are the key elements that should be covered in your brief for the profit improvement change initiative. We have already established the gaps in the organizational change success factors. We also have a specific and measurable outcome defined, but the brief should cover additional items such as the team leader, the team members, the time frame (suggested to be eight weeks normally), the resources available to the team, a nominated team sponsor, and a set date for reporting back recommendations to senior management. The clearer you can make the project brief, the more impact you will have on organizational change success factors such as need for change and change process.

Step 5—Plan the eight-week cycle. You should plan when your team (even if it is only a two-person team) will meet, where it will meet, how many people need to be present for a meeting to be held (quorum), and what will be done in each of the eight weeks. In a small business the process is much simpler to implement but the steps are the same. Our recommended structure is as follows:

Week 1—Confirm the project brief and key activities. Allocate the jobs to each team member or sub-team.
Week 2—Determine where we are now. Gather the data on where we are currently with the issue. In the example of the profit improvement team, you would gather data on the product, current sales, relevant overheads, pricing points, competitor analysis, estimated current profitability, sales and profitability trends, and the like.
Week 3—Determine where we want to be by the end of the calendar year. Defining the vision for profit improvement for year-end was part of our vision and it was specified to be a 25 percent increase over the current profitability. Any other detail that you could develop for the vision would provide increased clarity.
Week 4—Analyze the data. This week, team members should be analyzing the data as it comes in and ascertaining any elements that would impact, positively or negatively, our 25 percent profit increase goal. The more data, the better at this stage. We are only halfway through the team process, and data will continue to come in right until the end of the project at week eight.
Week 5—Draft the plan. Even though we have three weeks to go, I suggest you try and draft the plan now to identify what is still left to do. You should find there are several key elements of the plan missing, and you will have time to develop them. The data gathering and analysis from previous weeks can continue as this happens.
Week 6—Develop the solution. Now the rubber needs to hit the road. Even though the planning process continues, we have run

out of time if we are to achieve our eight-week goal. Now is the time to write up the plan.

Week 7—Design the presentation. No matter how clever and insightful your solution for achieving a 25 percent growth in profit, you need to be able to sell it to senior management. We suggest that you consider what the likely reaction to senior management will be and anticipate any objections to the design of your presentation. Make sure you cover the process you used as it will give senior management confidence that you have used the right process to achieve this outcome.

Week 8—Practice the presentation. I suggest that you presell your recommendations to any significant members of the senior management team before you do your presentation. Go to that person and say something like, "We are not sure we have this right; would you mind having a look at it and letting us know what you think?" If the senior management member comes back with any constructive criticism, you still have time to resolve any issues. If the feedback is all positive, then you can have the confidence that your presentation is likely to be well received. Make sure you rehearse the presentation a few times because every time you do it, you will get better. Why not videotape the final presentation so that you have a permanent record of your work and the reaction of senior management?

This process works for any size organization and any industry. The context in that I wrote this is more for a larger business, but it will still work perfectly for a micro business. A formal approach is much like a checklist; it makes sure that none of the vital steps are ignored.

Organizational Change Q&A

Things do not change; we change.

— *Henry David Thoreau*

As a consultant for over forty years to date, I have collected many questions from people desiring to change and improve their organizations. Hopefully the following list of commonly asked questions covers any concerns that you may have.

1. *How long should I give my change initiative team to complete their change initiative?*
   As I have already stated, an eight-week cycle is ideal. Eight weeks enables them to achieve a good outcome, hold their focus, and not overburden the already busy team members. If you allow them to take more time, I can assure you, they will take it! The problem with longer periods is that they compress the work at the start and then in the last few weeks before they are due to present their findings. The hiatus in the middle is extremely wasteful and risks the team losing momentum and commitment.
2. *Do I need to train each of the team members?* I strongly encourage you to do just that, unless you have people within the team skilled

and experienced in team and problem-solving tools and processes. If you rely just on debate as your change tool, you will end up with a much of the same outcome, a rearranging of the deckchairs. Using continuous improvement tools, such as a force field, five whys, and a decision matrix, always results in team synergy and innovative solutions.

3. *What happens if the team hits a roadblock?* This is normally an opportunity for team sponsors to reinforce that they are there to help. Probably the worst roadblock you can experience is when the team leader selected initially proved to be ineffective. It is embarrassing to have to make a change halfway through the process, but this can be done sensitively by moving the team leader out under the guise of needing him or her on another project or special task. Before getting to this drastic action, I would suggest that the team leader is coached to success. This infers that the team sponsor keeps a close watch on proceedings and can identify when the team starts moving off track.
4. *Is one team enough or do I need more?* In a larger organization I would use multiple teams, mainly because this increases the probability of success of one or more teams. In a small organization, you are often confined to just one team due to the limited size of the organization. In that case, you need to be far more vigilant to make sure that the single team is successful. The benefit in a large organization is that the multiple teams can be allowed to succeed or fail to allow some assessment on the culture of the organization. It is critical that at least one or more teams do succeed in this situation.

Part B—Personal Change Success

Very often a change of self is needed more than a change of scene.

— *A. C. Benson*

Like Part A, Part B provides an overview in the form of an executive summary of the topic, a brief explanation of the research methodology (for those that are interested), a brief overview of the research literature around personal change, the change model that we developed, and then a detailed explanation of the nine personal change success factors. Using a case study methodology, the use of the diagnostic is demonstrated and strategies for implementing a personal change initiative are explained. This leads to other factors, such as how to measure your progress, the impact of personal change beliefs, barriers to change, and then a question-and-answer section. Using the content page, you can go straight to any section of specific interest; however, you may find you learn more by investing in reading Part B from beginning to end.

Personal Change Executive Summary

I have noticed even people who claim everything is predestined and that we can do nothing to change it, look before they cross the road.

— *Stephen Hawking*

Each of us contemplates a need for change in our lives daily. Many defer acting, in part because they lack the confidence in their ability to be successful with the proposed personal change initiative. Often people are happy with their lot in life and are not dissatisfied enough to want to change. They find it difficult to think of a change initiative that they consider important enough. The fact is there are no limitations on what this initiative can be. It can be something simple, such as learning a new skill, losing weight, undertaking professional development, taking an international trip, or even simply reading a book recommended by friend. This person's thought process generates messages such as "I won't be able to do that" or "I will do that at another time." Failure to act is an instant defeat of the proposed personal change initiative. Social media posts by others often lead people to think that they should be targeting some change, but they are wary of failing. A failure can confirm their poor self-esteem and lack of confidence. When they feel forced to attempt change, they often resort to a trial-and-error process with its resultant low probability of success.

The Mindshop organization conducts annual surveys of the current and emerging needs of its two main client segments: business advisors and business leaders. One of the underlying trends that we noticed in late 2018 was increased stress and reduced resilience reported from our clients about people in their organization and their clients and customers. We decided to research this issue with the aim of developing a personal change initiative success model that people could use to increase the probability of success with those initiatives.

The resultant model confirmed that the three factors of organizational change success of readiness, capability, and beliefs were equally applicable to personal change. This made sense because an organization is made up of individuals, each with personal change goals either in play, or being contemplated. The research process started with a pool of forty successful leaders from which we identified twenty exemplar leaders with above average personal change success. We then surveyed these leaders to find out which of the fifteen factors had the biggest impact on their personal success. This resulted in a model for personal change success comprising nine elements. The weighing of the nine elements confirmed that readiness and beliefs both contributed 36 percent to the overall change probability, with the remaining 28 percent due to capability.

A diagnostic to enable people to estimate their current start point on a personal change initiative and to identify gaps that are negatively impacting their personal change potential was developed. The overall change process was tested by me with good success. Global training of all the Mindshop advisers was conducted in February and March 2019, and this enabled distribution of the personal change initiative model and created feedback from the field on improvements, as well as confirmation that the model worked.

Part B of this book outlines the research methodology, the resultant personal change model, provides access to the personal change diagnostic, and outlines a process for implementing personal change. The barriers to change have been outlined, suggestions for improving each of the gaps identified through the diagnostic are provided, and answers are provided to any frequently asked questions.

Personal Change Research Process (Optional Reading)

Change your opinions, keep to your principles,
change your leaves, keep intact your roots.

— *Victor Hugo*

IF YOU ARE READING THE research process for the personal change success model, I can assume that you probably read the research process for organizational change success as well. The good news is much of the framework for organizational change applies to personal change; after all, an organization is made up of a whole lot of individuals undergoing continuous personal change.

My research on organizational change success, integrated with the excellent work of other researchers, led us to safely assume that change success had three major components: change readiness, capability, and belief systems. I assumed that this framework could be carried across, and the actual research question I wanted to answer became what is an individual who has achieved personal change success in their life doing that is different to most other people? My first challenge was to identify at least twenty people successful in implementing personal change initiatives.

What makes a person successful? One of the Mindshop tools we refer to is the life balance wheel. There are six parts to this wheel, and each needs to be evenly balanced. When I run through the six parts, consider how well you are doing in each. The key thing is the wheel balance, not the quantum of success in each component. You don't need a perfect score in each of the sectors. Like any wheel, balance is our goal. Once we have that, we can start working on increasing the size of the wheel and how fast it turns.

The first segment of the wheel I'll call social. Social includes friends, entertainment, fun, and family. Like many of the sectors of the wheel, there is some overlap of social with other sectors, which you will see as we work through them. The benefit of social life is fun and relaxation, but it often involves fitness and health issues. A person's social life varies at different stages of their life. As a child, social life is a very important part of your wheel. Play dates, sleepovers, and even school itself are parts of a child's social life. Research has found that as you age, family becomes even more important than friends. When I've wondered about that, I have concluded that one of the factors is that we are very time poor, so we give priority to family over friends. People with young children often find they are even more time poor, with a consequential reduction in their social life. How would you rate your social life on a scale between zero and ten, where zero is very bad and ten is very good?

Family is closely related to social, particularly early in life for most people. What normally bonds a family together that makes it special is love. Love is like a filter that enables you to see the best in a person and be less concerned about any annoyances. We normally don't have the love filter when we are dealing with most of the people in our life. Even though the relationships between family members is enhanced through love, these relationships cannot be taken for granted. Unless maintained, the strength of the relationships between individuals within the family can weaken. There are things that you can do to improve family relationships. These include forgiveness, quality time, and thoughtfulness. How would you rate your family life on a scale between zero and ten?

Health is a key area of the wheel and one that can vary throughout life. A younger person in perfect health thinks very little about health issues. Body shape may occupy their thoughts, but that is different from health. An elderly person with a whole range of health issues may find that a large part of their life is taken up with tests, doctor appointments, medicines, and keeping their friends up-to-date with their most recent ailments. In many cases, health is something you can work on. Keeping your weight under control, exercising, and generally keeping fit is within most people's control. The link between health and energy is interesting. We need energy to drive our wheel and my experience is the healthier you are, the more energy you have to drive that wheel. How would you rate your health on a scale between zero and ten?

The mental part of your life balance wheel involves developing your cognitive skills and experience. Many people undergo full-time education early in their life, and then at a certain point, they resort to the school of hard knocks from then on. They use a trial and error approach to learn new things, one inherently wasteful of time and energy. I am a believer in lifelong learning and have studied most of my life using a combination of academic training, reading and listening to books, and putting myself in situations where learning new things is one of the key outcomes. I like to remind people that formal study, such as attending courses and reading books is just the ticket to the game. The real education occurs through the application of that learning to the key elements of your life. My goal is to build my capability continuously regardless of my age. This takes a considerable investment but the return on investment can be significant. How would you rate your mental segment of your wheel on a scale between zero and ten?

Philosophy is a key segment of your wheel and can mean religion to some, spirituality to others, and beliefs to the rest. A common connection between people over the ages has been a belief in something. Of the three groups above, I consider myself to be spiritual. This is reflected in what I read and what I think about. It's what I read, think about, and experience that ends up being a belief. This doesn't mean I can't change my beliefs, as all these contributing factors influence me continuously. There is nothing better than reading an insightful book or meeting a challenging person, resulting in some modification of my philosophy about life. You can work on philosophy through these mechanisms, but who is to judge how well you are doing? The answer is you. How would you rate your philosophy on a scale between zero and ten?

Our final segment of our wheel is finance. I define rich as someone who spends less then they make. The finance segment of your wheel doesn't require you to be extremely wealthy but rich in accordance with my definition. How financially rich you are varies throughout your life. I remember as a young father struggling to make ends meet. This is because at that time what I was making was not sufficient to cover things like the house payment, food, clothing, and three children. Fortunately, as I got older, hopefully a bit more capable, the amount I make increased to where it did exceed my spending. Where are you in this continuum? How would you rate your finance on a scale between zero and ten?

Now that you understand the six life balance wheel elements, I can tell you that I used these and my knowledge of many people in Mindshop to select forty successful people to survey about their personal change initiatives. Of course, I knew more than forty, but I picked people who I knew would respond quickly and be open and honest with their opinions on the various personal change success elements in their life. I designed and applied questions around change readiness, capability, and beliefs to identify people who scored well on each of these change success factors.

The analysis of the scoring then identified twenty people who, through self-assessment, scored the highest of the forty originally surveyed. This group of twenty exemplars of personal change were then surveyed again. Each person was given a list of fifteen key factors covering change readiness, capability, and beliefs and were asked to rank their importance to a recent personal success initiative that they had undertaken. One person commented that the personal success initiative that she had in mind was the completion of an MBA. Others had used a fitness campaign, resolving a family problem, and even developing their personal capability in applying Mindshop tools and processes. It really didn't matter what the personal success initiative was; it was more about what they did to achieve a successful outcome.

The total weight of the 15 key factors gave us a priority list. By setting a cut-off point for relevancy of a score as having an above average weight of eight, it was clear that nine of them fell into this category and also fit well under the headings of change readiness, capability, and beliefs. We had our personal change success model and a good indication of how important each of the nine factors in the model are through spreading evenly (for simplicity) the factors against the percentage impact that segment had on personal change success. A simple research program, but one with great potential; now it needed to be tested! As we did for the organizational change success research, I invested time into finding scientific papers around personal change. Some of the most relevant were those I identified back in 2014 as part of my organizational change success research, but many were more recent, including some published in 2019. Integrating some of the findings of this independent research into my thinking assisted to confirm and explain our findings.

Personal Change Literature

Only the wisest and stupidest of men never change.

— CONFUCIUS

MY RESEARCH INTO PERSONAL CHANGE continues and I have made it a priority to continuously search academic databases for interesting new developments. I have selected a sample of the papers that have contributed to the knowledge base of personal change that I think will be of interest to you. A synopsis of each sample paper and its APA citation follows:

Tamir, L. M. & Finfer, L. A. (2016). Executive coaching: The age factor. *Consulting Psychology Journal: Practice and Research, 68(4),* 313-325. doi: 10.1037/cpd0000069

Lifespan psychology suggests that leaders in their 30s, 40s, and 50s represent different maturity and professional experience levels and respond differently to a typical executive coaching engagement. This study analyzed 72 executive coaching engagements to evaluate the relationship of age to four distinct variables, responsiveness, self-reflection, non-defensiveness, and degree of change.

Responsiveness was defined as the degree to which the executive appreciates the coaching opportunity and dedicates the time and energy required to achieve leadership development. Self-reflection was considered to encompass insight, self-examination, and the willingness to question and re-evaluate one's approaches and standards. Non-defensiveness is where a leader accepts responsibility for their role played in events and keeps the dialogue going even in the face of difficult content. The behavioral change was measured from the perspective of the organizational stakeholders and was operationalized as low, medium, or high.

The hypothesis of this study was that executives in their 30s would be more idealistic and rule-bound and prefer absolutes in ambiguity. This would differ from those in their 40s and 50s as it was thought that they would be less responsive because the executive coaching would challenge their rules, less self-reflective because they would be less likely to question their ideals, less non-defensive because they would struggle with the ambiguity, and less changeable because they would perceive that they are already earmarked as top talent in the organization.

The study found that self-reflection and degree of change increase with age. Skepticism, diligence, and dutifulness decreased with age. This suggested that as executives age, those who receive coaching become more open to criticism, are more flexible and less dependent on the approval of others. These results suggest that leaders in their 30s are less introspective and less amicable to profound change when compared to older executives. It is thought that they are more likely to miss subtlety and do not appreciate the power of nuance and paradox. The executives in their 40s and 50s have already learned from experience and are more likely to accept imperfection and ambiguity. The executives in their 30s are focused on establishing themselves and have little time or inclination for reflection.

Two approaches to assist with the executive coaching of the 30 to 39 group of executives were firstly, to improve self-reflection through orchestrating an intervention to confront the executive with the poor behavior perceived by others and an explanation of the consequence that can then follow. The second approach pinpoints degree of change. It requires formulating *if-then* scenarios. An example is when the executive is advised to let go of a conflict because they would be then more likely to build an advantageous relationship with the person they conflicted with. Executives in their 30s who receive coaching are just as motivated and enthusiastic about developing their skills as are older executives. They do not differ significantly from other age groups on responsiveness to the coaching opportunity nor are they outwardly defensive the challenges. It is just that they do not dig deep and are unlikely to do so without the prompting of one or both of these methods.

Converse, B. A., Juarez, L. & Henneke, M. (2018). Self-control and the reasons behind our goals. *Journal of Personality and Social Psychology: Personality Processes and Individual Differences.* doi: 10.1037/pspp0000188

Motivational theorists agree that successful goal pursuit is not just about what you are pursuing and how, but also why you are pursuing. People may work just as hard when they *have to* as when they *want to.* The intensity of motivation may be at similarly high levels, but if the reasons for this motivation are different, then it may take on a different quality.

Most people desire to pursue interesting work and make a meaningful contribution. Providing access to inherently interesting tasks and involvement in autonomy supportive situations can promote such an experience. People do not always have this luxury of optimal goal pursuit conditions. Self-control was found to help an individual to access these conditions. Self-control is a factor in recognizing the interesting features or higher level meaning of one's work. People with lower levels of self-control will find it more difficult.

Third parties wishing to help others achieve success may need to more actively shape the situation, emphasizing freedoms more, providing more opportunities for novelty, and helping to create the connection to higher level meaning. The research on self-regulation identifies self-control and self-determination as two major factors, however these areas rarely intersect. This study found that the quality of motivation may be determined not just by the features of the task and the situation but also by self-control processes initiated by the individual.

Previous research focused on how self-control makes goal pursuit easier by helping people to avoid temptations or by inflating the desirability of the end state. This research supports the premise of a link between self-control and autonomous motivation. The research indicates that individuals who are higher in self-control are tempted less frequently and less strongly to avoid their achievement goal. This suggests that those who are lower in self-control feel less autonomous motivation because they are feeling a stronger pull to do something else instead. Individuals who are higher in self-control will rely more on beneficial habits. These habits are automatic responses to an activating event. If an individual is prompted to access the quality of her motivation, but is unaware of why she is pursuing the specific goal, she may be more likely to infer that she must be pursuing it for intrinsic reasons. It appears that the quality of the motivation is the key success factor in the achievement of an objective.

Ebner, K., Schulte, E-M., Soucek, R. & Kauffeld, S. (2018). Coaching as stress management intervention: The mediating role of self-efficacy in a framework of self-management and coping. *International Journal of stress management, 25(3)*, 209-233. doi: 10.1037/str0000058

Coaching is defined as a confidential working alliance between a coach and a client focusing on their professional lives or problems impacting their vocational context. Coaching is a process that supports the client to find solutions and provides the client with tools to help them realize that solution. It is a facilitative intervention resulting in a change process. One of the hypotheses of this study was that coaching increases a participant's self-management skill. Another hypothesis was that coaching increases a participant's self-efficacy belief. The third hypothesis was that self-management is positively related to self-efficacy. The fourth hypothesis is that self-efficacy is positive related to the stress reducing coping strategies of situation control and social support and negative related to the stress enhancing coping strategies of rumination and avoidance. The final hypothesis was that self-efficacy mediates the relationship between self-management and situation control, social support, rumination, and avoidance.

The study confirmed that coaching has the potential to alter a client's self-efficacy beliefs. A model was developed for the relationship of self-management, self-efficacy, and strain (coping). The link between coping and strain helps explain the contribution of coaching on a participant stress reaction. Coaching strategies can be altered by enhancing self-management and self-efficacy. The possible benefits of coaching as a stress management intervention applies to both academic and business environments. Implementing coaching as a stress management intervention in organizations is recommended to address coordinative, financial, and HR related costs to ensure employees remain capable for working. This should reduce the reliance on third-party institutions to assist with organizational stress management structures. Fostering employee health using coaching may also enhance the organizational performance. Coaching may also hold pertinent benefits for organizations as an alternative to the traditional stress management training (which is largely avoided because of it stigmatizing character).

Personal Change Model

When you blame others, you give up your power to change.

— Robert Anthony

Having decided that the three key contributors to organizational change success—change readiness, capability, and the beliefs of the members of the organization—also applied to personal change success, the next step was to estimate what impact each of these factors had on the overall probability of personal change success. With some rounding of the numbers, it was determined from our survey results that change readiness and beliefs were 36 percent each, and the capability factor was only 28 percent. It was interesting to note that whereas in the organizational change success model capability was the biggest factor, in the case of the personal change success model, it was the least significant of the three core factors. Change readiness has four individual components: the need for change, vision, personal energy, and a plan. Capability had two parts: high-performance habits and perseverance. The three elements of beliefs were perceived benefits, self-confidence, and mindset. Each of these nine factors is explained in detail in the following chapters.

There are some interesting insights in the data we used to develop the personal change success model. Already mentioned is the fact that capability is now the least impactful key factor in personal change success. Talking to people about the model during the training that we provided globally on it early in 2019 confirmed our thoughts that with organizational change, you need other people's capability to assist you in creating change, but when considering personal change, you only need to consider your own capability. That reduced the importance of capability but did not remove it from the model.

Of the fifteen factors that our exemplars were asked to rank, the three that scored highest were perceived benefit of the change, need for change, and mindset. One could assume that the dissatisfaction that an individual has with their status quo, coupled with their vision of what it could be, provides the necessary fuel for the change, the required mindset, and the vital energy to drive that change to completion. The three factors that scored lowest were experience level, network, and the opinion and support of any significant others. This confirms our thought that collaboration with others becomes less important when undertaking a personal change. Every time I was questioned on the veracity of any of the scores in the model, I was able to remind people that the data is the data; don't shoot the messenger! Checking with our survey participants on the importance of significant others, we found that some people rated it highly and others considered it unimportant. I think it is much to do with what the change initiative is all about.

The diagram of the personal change success model follows:

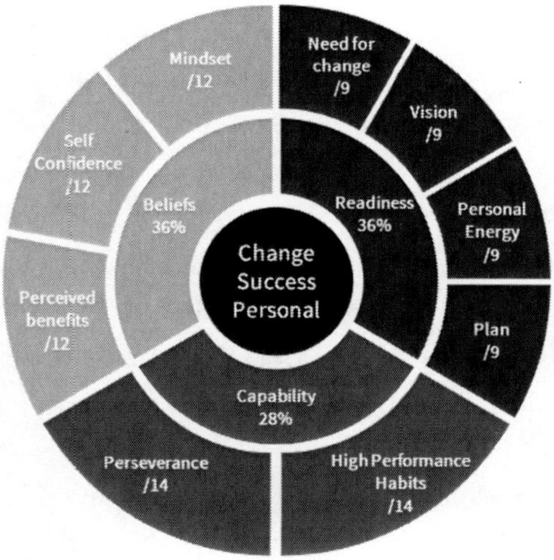

Personal Change Success Factor 1—Need for Change

Negative circumstances are catalysts for positive changes.

— Amanda L. Grossman

The need for personal change is a desire that needs to come from within. No one can force it on you. The key success element is contained in the word need. Need does not mean want. Need does not mean that someone else in your life wants you to do it. There is a sense of urgency with any need. You can feel that urgency; you must do it. It is not a should do or could do; it is a must! So how do you create that urgency? For me, it is because it is a contingent step in my purpose that is leading me to my vision.

Rather than wait in a reactive frame, a need requires you to drive it, to be proactive. If you do not take charge, then it is likely that no one else will. Only you will have the need and a willingness to satisfy that need. It is highly likely to require an investment, an investment of both time and energy. It will also require you to score well on each element of the personal change success model so that you maximize the probability of success of your change initiative. It is likely to require a revolution rather than an evolution. What step change will you need? Are you happy to wait until all the stars align and it just happens? Do you need to see every step of the process before you move? Are you willing to take a risk and start the journey not knowing every step required complete it?

I have always been the one to take the risk, confident in my ability to wing it no matter what barriers I faced along the way. I still have my own constraints. If I needed to become a medical doctor, I have a belief that it would be all too hard. Turning 70 this year makes me think that no university would accept me; it would take too long to get the experience I need to be a skilled doctor. I have given up before I even started. Thankfully, I didn't see it that way when I had a need to complete a PhD in psychology. I knew it would take eight years. I knew it would require an investment of thirty hours per week on top of my fifty hour per week job. I was confident that whatever barriers I encountered, I would find a way either over them, around them, or through them. This confidence did not come from previously completing a PhD. It came from my success at other studies, competing in athletics, maintaining friendships over a long period. In fact, for any activity that I felt a need for, I could see a track record for completing them successfully and overcoming any barriers. Your life will be much the same; the achievements may be different but just as valuable. The clarity of your vision is of prime importance at this stage. Rating your need for change out of nine, what score would you give to the need for change for your personal change initiative?

Personal Change Success Factor 2—Vision

There are two kinds of fools: those who can't change their opinions and those who won't.

—*Josh Billings*

THE CLARITY OF YOUR VISION of what will be the outcome of your change initiative is our first factor to consider. A practical way to commence the vision creation process is to attempt to mind map the elements of the future outcome. If your personal change initiative is the completion of an MBA, as an example, then the mind map may have arms on it representing things like job opportunities, pay level, respect of others, self-confidence, a sense of achievement, and even a tick off your bucket list. One of the benefits of a mind map is that can record both hard and soft outcomes. A standard practice with a mind map is to then Pareto it to find the key vision elements. As a reminder, the Pareto rule states that 20 percent of the elements of the mind map will create 80 percent of the benefit, in this case, clarity of your vision.

An associated vision creation process is the one we use for developing purpose. Most people understand the benefit of being able to define your purpose; I haven't found too many that have done it successfully. For those that have, their ability to determine whether the change initiative is a key success factor or not is enhanced. I was able to reveal my purpose (in life) back in 1994. I have not changed it since then. The elements of that purpose statement inform my vision. My overall vision then informs what change initiatives I need to be undertaking. There needs to be a clear link and synergy between my purpose, my overall vision, and the specific vision I have for my personal change initiatives.

I drafted my purpose statement on January 10, 1994, in the form of an *I am* statement. This statement was developing in my mind throughout the second half of 1993, and I used my vacation time in January to reflect on where I was heading. Seemingly from nowhere came the following statement:

I AM

- the best publisher of business and personal processes in the world
- a world citizen travelling and living wherever I can provide the maximum value to others
- a provider of support and inspiration to those closest to me, my family, and my friends
- continuously developing my skills, knowledge, and understanding through trust in myself
- prospering and sharing my wealth and happiness with others and so rewarding myself

This purpose statement has been framed and is hanging on a wall in the Mindshop head office and in my home office. It is a constant reminder of my purpose in life and it enables me to see what I do and what I don't do.

I developed a simple process for revealing your purpose. An assumption in this process is that you are already on purpose. What has happened to you in the past has nudged you to where you are today. Once I realized that everything, both positive and negative (in my perception anyway), has been equally valuable to me in heading towards my ultimate purpose, I decided that rather than letting events push and pull me as I had done in the past, going forward I would decide what factors would head me more efficiently toward my purpose. The process involves writing a sentence for where you are today about things like your family, friends, education, money, career, in fact anything that you think is important. It is difficult to write a single sentence on something as important as your family.

Once you have drafted a sentence for today on each of your chosen factors, now go back five years and repeat the process. Where were you five years ago? How would you describe each of your chosen factors in a sentence for five years ago? Once you've done that, go back another five years, and then another five years. Keep going until you can't remember any further details. You will be surprised how far you can go back. Depending on how old you are, you will have all your key factors described in a sentence at five-year intervals. Stand back from your life, digest all the information you have written, and see if you can identify any patterns. You should start seeing linkages between events. You should also be able to identify through a Pareto analysis which of these are the most significant in you being where you are right now. You should find that the negative events have had just as positive impact on your current position as any positive ones.

Now for the tricky part. Can you extrapolate this data and see where you are heading? The extrapolated goodness of fit line should be pointing straight at your purpose. If it doesn't, it may mean that you need to dig down into your past and present and create more detail. For a young person, that can mean writing sentences for your key factors at two-year intervals rather than five. Don't get frustrated with the process; it is a good idea after you finish writing and contemplating the patterns to put it aside and let your subconscious work on all the linkages for you. When you are ready, the purpose will pop into your mind, just like mine did.

If you re-examine my purpose statement, you will see that it starts painting a picture of my future. If I did a mind map purely based on my purpose statement, it would have arms such as international travel, friends, family, capability, sharing, wealth, support, value, and trust. I can see each of those elements. I can see me connected to each. A vision, by definition, means you can see it. If you can see it, you can get it. If you can't see it, it will be difficult, if not impossible, to get. How would you score yourself for vision in the personal change success model? The maximum score for vision is nine points. If you can develop a high score for vision, it will automatically generate energy for you to invest in bridging the gap between where you are now and where the vision sees you in the future.

Personal Change Success Factor 3—Personal Energy

What we change inwardly will change outer reality.

— *Plutarch*

Your overall personal energy and the amount of energy that you are willing to apply to your change initiative determine whether you will be successful. You can develop high energy levels by being fit and healthy and not wasting energy. You need to have spare energy in case you experience any barriers to your change process. If the personal change initiative excites you, when you spend time on it, you find that time just evaporates, and you feel it is one of the highest priorities in your life. That excitement will generate energy for your project. You can feel when you are in the flow or not. When you are in the flow, everything works for you; barriers disappear, and support and encouragement are plentiful. The people around you can also either contribute to or erode your energy levels. It is essential that you avoid any energy vampires.

You can tell an energy vampire by how you feel after spending any time with them. Even a few minutes can make you feel drained. That should be your trigger to move on, to find someone else who is an energy giver not an energy vampire. You are better off on your own than spending time with an energy vampire. There are several ways that people can steal energy from you. In *The Celestine Prophecy* written by James Redfield, he suggests the people that steal energy are intimidators, interrogators, "poor me," and aloof. The intimidators are the bullies that you know. They intimidate you to put you on the defensive; in that way, they keep control of you. The interrogators ask you lots of questions but to keep you off balance. The "poor me" people spend all their time telling you their woes in the hope that by feeling sorry for them, you will give them energy. The aloof person makes you take the first move in the relationship. These people subconsciously believe that this puts you in a weaker position than them.

We can use each of these four profiles when it suits us. The profile that I am most likely to revert to is being aloof. I justify in my mind using the excuse that I don't want to impose myself on someone. Even though I am aware of this tendency, I regularly catch myself outdoing it in some circumstances. I have noticed that it is more likely to happen when I'm meeting new people. If I don't get a good feeling about someone at that initial meeting, my aloof tendency normally continues with them from then on. I have reflected on this, and I'm yet to discover what the specific triggers are. Which profile of energy vampire are you most likely to use, and under what circumstances?

I find if I try to get to know someone and not be too quick in judging them, I am more likely to not revert to aloof mode. If you have read the section on biases in Part A of this book, you will be aware of how biases can distort the accuracy of your perceptions. There is another list of biases in Part B of the book; these are even more relevant to personal change. The closest I've got to understanding my behavior is that I could be competitive with new people that I perceive to be capable business people. If I sense that I'm starting to revert to aloof, I tell myself that this person will be very interesting and that I should take the time to find out what is unique about them. This simple technique seems to distract the aloof behavior and replace it with genuine interest.

When people are considering whether to make a change in their personal lives and are questioning whether to invest energy into it, I always remind them that it costs more energy to not change than it does to make the change. The problem with my argument is that it is hard to quantify concurrently the two options of changing or not changing. I then remind the person that I am talking to that in nature, you are either growing (changing) or you are dying (not changing). When you look at a living thing, such as a bush or a tree, there are usually bits of the bush or tree that are dead, but most of it is growing and is very healthy. When you stand back far enough, what do you see? You will see a healthy bush or tree; you hardly notice the bits that are dying. This is much like a person. Old habits die, and new habits flourish. A healthy tree normally has good access to nutrients. A healthy, growing, energetic person also has access to the right nutrients. Depending on what your change initiative is, you may need to supplement these nutrients.

Your nutrients may include eating well, controlling your weight, avoiding energy vampires, mixing mostly with energy givers, as well as adding knowledge, experience, skills, and your focused attention. As you have seen in the personal change success model, change readiness is 36 percent of the potential probability of change success. The more we can invest in developing and focusing our energy, the higher the probability of our change initiative. How would you rate yourself in terms of personal energy and the amount of that energy that you are willing to invest in your proposed personal change initiative? With a potential score of nine, what score would you give your personal energy that you can apply to your personal change initiative? You will need a high score here to invest in your plan for change.

One challenge you are likely to have is to be able to generate sufficient energy for your chosen personal change initiative. It would be unwise to expect that you had the energy and resources for one hundred needs. Too many people spread themselves very thinly and take on too many concurrent tasks. They do none of these tasks well, and it negatively impacts on their self-confidence. You need to guard your valuable energy and only invest it on the things of most need, those things that take you toward your purpose and fit clearly with your vision.

Personal Change Success Factor 4—Plan

It is not the strongest or the most intelligent who will survive, but those who can best manage change.

— *Charles Darwin*

When people complete our personal change success diagnostic, in many cases, the personal change success factor that has the biggest gap between where the person self-assesses their current performance and a perfect score for the factor, it is the plan that seems to be their biggest opportunity for improvement. The plan has primarily two key ingredients: a strategy that describes how they will achieve their personal change initiative and the action plans that will enable them to deliver that strategy successfully. The action plans need to address any skills that need to be improved or developed to have the capability to implement these actions.

The plan has three key sections: the now, the where, and the how. The now section can be a simple list of bullet points that state where the person is now on their selected change initiative. If a person's objective is to lose weight, then it may be bullet points around current weight, current exercise program, current calorie intake, and where the individual's weight has been trending line over the last years. The where section lists in bullet points where the person wants to be at some future point (say six months), how he or she will look and feel, and maybe even a list of benefits that that will be gained upon hitting that target weight. The where section may even include some key performance indicators (KPIs) that will show how well the action plans have been implemented. The final section of the plan is the how. This is where the rubber hits the road. It will list all the actions that need to be put in place and implemented to achieve the gap between the now and the where. In our weight loss example, it could be a plan to increase calorie burn and reduce calorie intake. KPIs would be a useful addition to the how plan, but they would focus less on outcomes and more on the process. The process for weight loss could include daily measuring of weight, steps taken, distance travelled, calories burned, body mass index (BMI), body fat percentage, in fact, anything that would help confirm whether the plan is working or not. If we find the plan is not working, then all we need to do is try a different action. Working harder on a plan that is not achieving your KPIs is not a recommended automatic first step. My preference is to do more of what works and try different things for what is not working.

Part of the plan will be developing strategies and actions to build the required skills that will be needed for your proposed personal change initiative. These skills may be general skills, such as time management, problem-solving, and decision-making. They are also likely to be more specific, subject matter expert, skills closely related to the project that you have chosen. It is generally a combination of both types of skills that you will need to develop to be successful with your change initiative.

The key advantage of a written plan is that it can be shared with others. It can be shared at the drafting stage with people who would have the right knowledge and experience to suggest improvements to make sure we are planning the right implementation strategy. Another benefit of sharing the written plan is that can be used by trusted people to help us with the accountability of sticking to the plan. I always tell people what I am planning to do because I find it adds to my perseverance. I never want to admit that I have given up on something due to the lack of effort. This reinforces the importance of process KPIs that will tell us whether we are on track or not. Asking someone to buddy with you is also a good idea for accountability. How would you rate your plan—it's out of nine—for your personal change initiative? If you can achieve a high score for plan, we will need to have high-performance habits to ensure we implement the plan successfully.

Personal Change Success Factor 5—
High-Performance Habits

What we achieve inwardly will change outer reality.

— *Plutarch*

HIGH-PERFORMANCE HABITS, BY OUR DEFINITION, focus mainly on time management and discipline. We could have included additional habits such as working long hours, doing what you say when you say you will, and asking for help when you are stuck. I think that these habits can be assumed. They may be areas that you could do better, but most people who have the energy to read this book will normally have good performance habits in any case. They may also be disciplined and good with time management, but are they consistent in how they apply these habits?

One high-performance habit that I have created is all about stress management. As stress increases on us, often our performance increases, but when it gets to a point where the performance plateaus, we can hit a point which psychologists call free-floating anxiety. This is where people will either overreact or underreact when faced with issues. I can tell when I am getting close to this zone, and I know that the only way to deal with it is to wind back the stress on myself. Having some time off, exercising, avoiding alcohol, and spending time on less arduous tasks all help reduce stress levels. Creating time for tasks that I enjoy helps reduce the stress.

When you are already very busy, it is quite difficult to create additional time and energy to achieve new goals, even if they are important ones. It is a problem that most leaders have that they have trouble letting go. For whatever psychological reasons, they think they can keep adding more things to do into the constraint we all share of only having 168 hours at our disposal each week. No one in the world gets more than you do, but I am probably safe to say that some people make better use of their 168 hours than you do.

The process that allows you to keep adding new and important tasks into your 168 hours a week is a simple one. We have previously used the Pareto rule. We are about to use it again. This time I suggest that you think about the 20 percent of things that you do with your 168 hours per week that are creating 80 percent of the benefit you are to the world (probably your work colleagues and family will do for this calculation). Make a list of those high-value things that you are currently doing. This means that 80 percent of the things you do with your 168 hours is creating far less benefit. Make a list in descending order of value of all these items in your 80 percent of where your time goes. Only list the big items; you don't need to list things like cleaning your teeth or feeding the dog. In this descending list of value that you are currently investing time in, pick the bottom five to ten items on the list. Work out how you could either stop doing them or delegate them. Maybe even using technology could remove some of your low-value activities. Give yourself just a few weeks for the first item and see what you can do to either remove it or diminish its impact on your 168 hours. Keep repeating the process until the degree of difficulty in removing items becomes a barrier. You may be pleasantly surprised to find that you can free up as much as ten hours per week using this process.

Assuming we have created ten hours in this way, how can we invest that time more wisely? We could use it to work on our personal change initiatives. We could spend more time with our families. We could spend more time on developing our capability. How would you like to spend this time to improve your life? I have a practice of doing this annually and have maintained the discipline of doing it for decades. At the end of each calendar year, I start thinking about what I can either delegate or stop doing. In the early days, I could create as much as a 50 percent vacuum in my life, which I then filled with exciting and interesting new tasks. Removing the drudgery of my week gave me more energy and removed clutter from my vision for the future. Having more short-term success encouraged me to better persevere with my plans. For your proposed personal change initiative, how would you score your high-performance habits? The maximum score available is fourteen points. This is one of the most critical success factors in the whole personal change model, but without perseverance of your high-performance habits, you will find it difficult to succeed. If it is a habit, it does suggest that you will persevere, for what happens if you hit any unexpected barriers?

Personal Change Success Factor 6—Perseverance

The question isn't who is going to let me; it's who is going to stop me.

— *Ayn Rand*

How persistent and tenacious are you? The quotation of Ayn Rand above, one of my favorite authors by the way, suggests that no one should be able to stop you from achieving the vision of your personal change initiative. Sometimes I think is better to not be overly smart; that way you don't know when to stop. Persistency and tenaciousness are closely related. It is a common success factor of successful people, and this importance is reflected in our model allocating 14 percent of the score for personal change success to this key capability factor.

I need to reinforce the point that I made earlier that trying harder at an incapable system is a stupid thing to do. A better approach would be to do more of what works and try a different approach to something that is not working. If you are trying to improve your golf game and that is the personal change initiative you have selected for the next eight weeks, you may have selected as part of your plan to get some professional coaching. If you find that this is not working, then it makes more sense to change your coach rather than give up on coaching altogether.

Part of perseverance is overcoming the self-doubt that can creep into your mind when, deep down, you know you haven't worked hard enough to achieve your targeted goal. When you feel that you deserve to succeed, then you probably will. When things come too easily, they don't feel right, in my experience, because they are not right! You can fool others most of the time, but you can't fool yourself. How often do you hear someone say, "Yes, I did get lucky, but it took me 20 years." Masterpieces take time is another of my favorite sayings and beliefs. I like the fact that as I get older, I seem to have more success. In part, this is because I have persevered with many of the important things in my life. That doesn't mean that I occasionally put things down, leave them for a while, and then pick them up again. I find that my subconscious working on problems and opportunities ensures that, over time, I do come up with more insightful solutions and ideas. Part of my perseverance is reflection.

I mentioned in one of the other factors about the role of a buddy. I've also mentioned how factors can overlap, much like a Venn diagram. None of the nine factors of personal change success are mutually exclusive. I think a buddy can help us in every factor but more so in the perseverance factor. Give your buddy permission to hold you accountable, to encourage you, to motivate you on your off days. It is not realistic to expect that you are one hundred percent on your game every day of your life. Sometimes some things need to be delayed for other things to fall into place for you. I'm not sure how this works, but there seems to be some structure to our lives which enables us to be successful.

Reflect on your perseverance in the past. Do you think that you have had the ability to be tenacious and persevere even when things are stacked against you? If you can think of occasions where you did, this is a good sign that you will do the same for this personal success change initiative. It is equally the most important single factor in the whole model, so you need to get this right. I would say that if you feel that this will be a difficult area, you maybe need to either make sure you can get good scores in the other eight factors, or even delay this initiative and select another. How would you rate your perseverance out of fourteen for your proposed personal change initiative? To enable a high score for perseverance, you will need to be convinced that there is going to be a personal benefit for you in due course.

Personal Change Success Factor 7—Perceived Benefits

I alone cannot change the world, but I can cast a stone across the waters to create many ripples.

— Mother Teresa

What will you gain from achieving your proposed personal change initiative? You need to understand what's in it for you. This factor is also one of the ten organizational change success factors. These are future benefits that are above and beyond anything you are enjoying now. The emphasis is on future. It is almost like your own perception of the return on investment (ROI) that you expect to get once you are successful with the personal change initiative. It's not a purely mathematical calculation by the way; you look at all the benefits that you think you may get and then divide those by all the inputs you need to invest. Unless you can see an ROI, the perceived benefits will not be significant enough to tap the 12 percent of the probability of personal change success that this factor should give you.

Why wouldn't you mind map all the benefits? We found earlier that a map is a great tool for capturing the tangible and soft benefits in any situation. Share the mind map with your buddy; see if they can think of any other benefits. The plan that you have developed for the personal change initiative should clearly define the inputs that you will need to make. Be careful to accurately estimate both the benefits and the inputs. Remember the optimism bias in Part A. If you go back and review optimism bias, take the time to skim over all the others just to make sure that you are seeing this ROI calculation realistically.

We do recommend that the duration of your personal change success initiative is relatively short, usually as short as eight weeks. This enables you to hold a focus, maintain your energy, but even so, you may need some short-term rewards before you can achieve the longer-term benefits from the initiative. Why wouldn't you consider a movie or a dinner at the halfway point? If you hit one of your key process KPIs along the way, reward yourself. You need to make sure that you feel that you deserve this reward because rewarding yourself without justification is obvious, at least to you! Can you clearly identify the perceived benefits (and ROI) for your proposed personal change initiative? For this factor the maximum score is twelve points. How confident are you that you can achieve the maximum score?

Personal Change Success Factor 8—Self-Confidence

Don't fear change, change fear.

— Nelson Mandela

Self-confidence underpins many of the other personal change success factors, such as perseverance, high-performance habits, and personal energy. Your trust in your abilities, qualities, and judgement, particularly in areas that are new to you, are components of self-confidence. The self-confidence needs to be realistic; otherwise, it becomes overconfidence. This is where your buddy can provide grounding on your capability and resultant confidence levels.

Self-confidence becomes of vital importance when you experience setbacks of any kind. It is a good rule to remember that things that fail teach you something. The successes are a form of rewards and encouragement that can boost self-confidence; the failures should also positively impact your self-confidence because they add to the experience and knowledge about whatever you're working on. This increased knowledge should boost self-confidence. To remind you of this, why not keep a journal of your project, recording the events, the successes, the failures, and your experiences. If nothing else, it will be interesting reading a few years down the track. I used to keep journals and did so for decades, and it was quite cathartic to one day go to my recycling depot and put every journal into the waste paper bin. It was a confirmation that the past was only relevant in building my confidence and capability to their current levels, and my focus needed to be fully on today and the future.

We talked earlier about energy vampires. Energy vampires can have a detrimental impact on your self-confidence whether you believe what they say or not. We all have some degree of self-doubt, and any criticism can either damage, or at least crack, our self-confidence. This can be repaired, but it's better to avoid the damage in the first place by avoiding the energy vampire or anyone who is negative. There is still a reserved place for trusted and respected people who give you constructive criticism. You can tell it's constructive when they point out a blemish but then suggest ways to fix that problem. They may even offer to help you by opening doors for you, providing resources, or assisting you in implementing your plan. Don't be reticent about asking for help.

I recognized very early in my career that I did have trouble asking for help. I love helping others, but for some reason, I find it difficult to accept help. I notice it in different ways. If I'm out for dinner with friends, I like to pick up the bill. I do know that they may also like to pay, but I push that to one side and rush to the credit card machine, often feigning some reason for having to leave the table. People often compliment me on my coaching ability and then go on to ask, "And who coaches you?" My standard answer is Emerson, Napoleon Hill, Wayne Dyer—in fact, lots of different authors, many of whom have passed away. I do watch and listen to any good operators and thinkers I meet, and there are lessons to be learned from each one of them. I learn just as much from other people's failures as I do their successes, much as I do with myself.

Self-confidence needs to constantly improve because the issues that you are addressing are normally increasing in complexity and difficulty. One way of building self-confidence is to experience a winning situation. When I coach people and I sense that they need to build self-confidence, I normally find that they are attempting to fix issues that are currently beyond them, out of their reach. I normally then get them to reset and take on fewer complex matters that can be guaranteed successes, particularly with my help, and through successes, they build a safety margin around their self-confidence. In parallel to this, I can loan them some of my self-confidence by offering my help. I normally preface my offer with words like "Between us, there is nothing that we can't fix on this project." How would you rate your self-confidence about your proposed personal change initiative? The maximum available score is twelve points. Self-confidence is significantly impacted by your mindset.

Personal Change Success Factor 9—Mindset

If you don't like something, change it. If you can't change it, change your attitude.

— *Maya Angelou*

Having the right mindset involves thinking positively about how much you desire your proposed outcome and the opinions and subsequent behaviors that you utilize to achieve your goal. Carol Dweck in her book, *Mindset*, defines a fixed mindset as our character, intelligence, and our creative ability. These components are largely fixed. What is changeable are things like our ability to grow through our challenges and seeing failures as an opportunity to learn and grow. These elements form part of our growth mindset.

Our biases as listed in both Part A and Part B of this book also impact our mindset. Get into the habit of listening to yourself and you will quickly see if you have any irrational beliefs. One of the Mindshop tools, which we call the belief behavior model, will help you reprogram any such beliefs. The belief behavior model is based on cognitive behavior theory, but I think our version is easier to understand. It works like this: we are all subjected to what I call *activating events* each day. An activating event can be something like getting stuck in traffic, having an argument with one of your children, or even having a performance management interview with your boss. We normally have little, if any, control over what activating events we need to deal with and when they occur. Our reaction to the activating event is to trigger some predetermined belief. As an example, the performance management interview with your boss may trigger a belief that "I am going to be criticized and she won't listen to me." If that is your belief, it automatically drives your behavior, which is likely to be defensive and to experience some anxiety. This behavior may subconsciously impact your boss, and she is likely to react (due to her irrational beliefs) in an equally defensive and anxious way, resulting in a consequence that is a disappointment for both of you. This is a recipe for disaster!

Fortunately, there is a solution to this dilemma. The only variable in the activating event-belief-behavior-consequence process is the belief. What if you reprogrammed your belief from "I am going to be criticized and she won't listen to me" to "This will be great; I will enjoy getting feedback on my performance'" What would that do to your behavior? I would think that it would cause you to be energized, open-minded, and willing to accept any constructive feedback. You may even feel that you have a choice whether to fully accept all the criticism or not. The consequence will be far more positive and one that will encourage both of you to have more open and honest conversations.

In my earlier career as a consultant, I had a mindset that restricted my personal success. In hindsight, I can see that it was a fear of success. I had a concern that too much success may have a negative impact on my family. At that time, I linked personal success to how hard I worked. Subconsciously, I believed that if I worked one hundred hours a week, then I would be twice as successful as I would if I worked fifty hours. I had completely missed the point around leverage, and at the same time I had a conflict between wanting to succeed and not wanting to damage my family. Thankfully, my wife took over the role of managing the family, which mitigated any risk that I would have caused in my hunter-gatherer perception of my role in the family. I'm not sure what triggered my change in beliefs around my role and work ethic, but I eventually did work out how to achieve the results of a hundred-hour week but only working fifty hours.

Think about someone who you know whom you consider to be highly successful. On what basis are you measuring that person's personal success? What have you observed about his or her mindset? When I think about people whom I consider to be highly successful, I think their mindset has elements of caring for others, doing what they say when they say they will do it, and being easy to deal with and trustworthy. The mindset of trustworthiness is interesting. It doesn't mean only trusting an individual on an ethical basis. I know if I left my wallet on our lunch table, it would still be there when I came back. With a highly successful person, trust also means that I can trust the person's capability, willingness to help me, reliability, and values. This is a full definition of trust. Successful people have chosen this mindset and this consequential behavior; that is why they are so successful. Scoring yourself out of twelve, how would you rate yourself on the mindset factor?

Look back over all nine of the personal change success factors. Adding up the scores will give your total probability of success for the personal change initiative you have in mind. If it is less than 80 percent, you can go back over the nine factors and determine specifics strategies and action plans for increasing each of the scores. Once you are confident that you have the strategies defined to boost your score to at least 80 percent probability, then make a start! Reflect on what you learn along the journey and adapt your strategies if you are still not achieving your goals.

Case Study—Personal Change Success

Change is such hard work.

— *Billy Crystal*

In early 2019 when we finalized the personal change success model, I decided we needed to test the veracity of the model on a real-life situation. I was excited at the prospect of being able to fix a personal issue in my life. Like most people, I had plenty of options to consider. On January 1, New Year's Day, I found my project—my weight. A less disciplined lead-up to Christmas and a relaxing family-orientated Christmas-New Year holiday meant that my scales registered 96.0 kg (211 lb.)—not a lifetime record, but much higher than my 85 kg (187 lb.) of just a few years before. I had been measuring my weight daily when at home for around five years, so the graph of my weight over that period confirmed a sine wave of highs and lows with a trend line clearly on the ascendant. Extrapolating that line into the future was pointing to potential health and energy problems as I headed into my seventies.

I reflected on the nine key success factors of the personal change success model and how they would help me get back to my ideal weight. I reviewed each of the nine factors as follows:

1. **Need for Change**. It was clear that I needed to reduce my weight significantly but also stop the sine wave of feast and famine.

The scale showed me there was a definite need for change. I could even quantify that need; it needed to be 8 kg (18 lb.).

2. **Vision**. The vision was easy to create because I had been at 88 kg before, just not over a year. The important part of my vision was the extra element about not being a weight outside the range of 87 kg to 89 kg. Reducing my weight to 88 kg was the easy part; staying within the range would be my challenge this time.
3. **Personal Energy**. This was an easy one because I have a habit of putting enough energy into anything I put my mind to. I was confident that I would do what I say, particularly if I communicated to the significant people in my life that this is what I would be doing.
4. **Plan**. I needed a plan that covered the input of calories and the expenditure of calories. Common sense told me that I would only lose weight if I used more calories than I input. On the input side, I decided to fast on most days (my vision was at least five days a week) for 20 hours. That meant I had a four-hour window in which I could input any food. Looking at my schedule, I could see that the five days per week goal would be achievable; in fact, most weeks I could probably hit the goal on every day of the week. If I was careful, it meant that my input would be around 750 calories per day. The second part of the plan was the expenditure of calories. I set an increased goal for burning calories on my Apple watch, set a thirty-minute-per-day exercise target, and this enabled me to estimate that I would burn around 2,500 calories per day. My plan was to have a 1,750 calorie deficit each day.
5. **High-Performance Habits**. Reflecting on how I'd fit my plan into my day, I realized that I couldn't guarantee that every day I could walk enough to hit my calorie expenditure goal. My plan B was to use my walking machine in my garage at the end of the day to ensure that I hit my goal. To make it a little easier, I set the goal as being for five days of the week.
6. **Perseverance**. I guess this is related to the high-performance habits and personal energy, but I was very confident that I would

see the plan out over the projected eight-week period. On reflection, the plan to drop weight at a rate of 1 kg per week (2.2 lb.) provided continuous reward for my effort. After just a few weeks, I could see the difference and that reinforced my perseverance.

7. **Perceived Benefits**. I decided that having more energy, fitting into my clothes, being healthier, and doing what I said I would do would be more than enough reward. I expected that I would know within the first week whether this was going to be difficult or not. It proved to be easy.
8. **Self-Confidence**. Because I'd done the weight-loss process before, I was confident that I could do it again. The difference this time was to include an additional process loop where if I went back up to 89 kg, it would trigger me to introduce my plan again, maybe just for a week or two, to get me back under 88 kg. I was confident that I would get down to 88 kg and then stay there.
9. **Mindset**. I was also confident in the mindset that I had and how that thought process would help me achieve my goal. After all, it was only for eight weeks; anyone could do it!

Having established that I could do well on all nine factors, I was ready to go. I manually completed the personal change success diagnostic scoring myself for where I was on January 1 and then where I wanted to be by February 26. The biggest gaps in my scoring were in the areas of vision, plan, and mindset. Each of these needed extra steps to ensure I achieved a maximum score in each. The vision's additional requirements included the maintenance mechanism to keep myself in the range between 87 kg and 89 kg, the increase in calorie burn through setting new targets on my Apple watch, and then accepting that I couldn't achieve these targets daily (sometimes life would get in the way), I modified the target to five days out of seven each week.

With the plan, it was just a matter of documenting the vision I have just described. The mindset was just as simple; I decided that I needed to ignore anyone's claim that the twenty hours daily fast was unhealthy. I researched twenty-hour fasting, found it had a name, the Warrior Diet, and found a book on intermittent fasting by Dr. Michael Mosley and Mimi Spencer. The research indicated that such a long fast would not be for everyone, but I was confident I could manage whatever happened. My nine factors indicated I was well above an 80 percent probability of success for my personal change initiative of losing 8 kg in eight weeks. I was ready to go!

Eight weeks later, I hit my target weight but decided to keep going for a ninth week just to make sure. My maintenance plan safety net was in place; now it was time to think about the next project. I liked the outcomes of my first eight-week cycle and I decided to then pick another topic and then repeat the eight-week cycle, indefinitely working on things for me or things for others. The second project was to complete this book by April 23. I felt that with two successful eight-week cycles under my belt, I would have proven the personal change success model.

I started to get excited. If we fixed a key personal issue every 8 weeks, what would my life be like in 12 months? Fix an issue, create a habit, lock it down, and then work on something new. I started to think about anything that could create a barrier to this vision.

Personal Change Diagnostic

We cannot change anything until we accept it.
Condemnation does not liberate, it oppresses.

— *Carl Jung*

As we did for the organizational change diagnostic, we will provide the personal change diagnostic in two forms: a manual version and an online version. Mindshop people can access the diagnostic through a web-based link on their coaching platform, and we have provided a general link below for you as well. When you complete the diagnostic, you will be required to enter an email address so that you can immediately receive a report on what your key issues are. For those not wanting to do this, we have also provided a hardcopy version that you can score manually. The link to the online version of the personal change success diagnostic follows: https://www.web.mindshop.com/change-success-personal-diagnostic/

You can also manually score the nine personal change elements to identify any gaps and your current probability of success for implementing a change initiative in the template following. As for the organizational change success diagnostic in Part A, the nine key elements of the personal change initiative diagnostic are listed under the headings of readiness, capability, and beliefs. The maximum weight for each of the elements are shown; for example, the need for change has a maximum score of 9 percent. Simply estimate where you are now in terms of your proposed personal change initiative on each of the nine elements calculating your score for readiness, capability and beliefs. The total score is your current probability of success in achieving that personal change initiative. What strategies and actions can you develop to ensure that your probability is at least 80 percent?

Factors		Now	Where	Gap	Strategy
READINESS 36%	Need for change		9		
	Vision		9		
	Personal Energy		9		
	Plan		9		
	Total		36		
CAPABILITY 28%	High performance habits		14		
	Perseverance		14		
	Total		28		
BELIEFS 36%	Perceived benefits		12		
	Self Confidence		12		
	Mindset		12		
	Total		36		
Total			100		

All you need to do is then integrate these strategies and actions into your current plan, and you can be confident of a successful outcome.

Keep in mind that most people are attempting their personal change initiatives with a probability of success by default in the range of 30 percent to 50 percent. You now have an 80 percent probability of success on paper with your strategies developed; now it's time to put the plans into action!

Personal Change Beliefs

Progress is impossible without change, and those who cannot change their minds cannot change anything.

— GEORGE BERNARD SHAW

IN PART A OF THIS book, I list eighteen biases that can be observed in organizations by studying the people who work in those organizations. I have listed below some more that I think are found in the general population and not just organizations. If you are aiming to create personal change in yourself or others, then understanding these biases will be essential.

Cultural bias: Cultural bias occurs when a person of a specific culture makes assumptions about others from a different culture based on his or her own cultural expectations. With the impact of globalization on the world, we are needing to interact with people of different cultures far more frequently than we have done in the past. The beliefs, norms, and practices of an individual can be determined by their culture and family upbringing. We should not assume that our beliefs, norms, and practices will apply to others. **Decline bias**: At my age, I hear a lot of my friends reminiscing about the good old days. Decline bias is a bias in favor of the past over what is currently happening or is likely to happen in the future. This is often a reflection that the person does not like change. We would like our world to make sense to us; when it changes, it is harder for us to understand. In part, we react like this when we are cognitively lazy.

Fundamental attribution error: We often tend to label people too quickly. Once labeled, the labels are hard to erase. We assume that a person's behavior is who they really are. If a person does something bad, then he or she must be a bad person, forever.

Self-serving bias: If you've noticed, when people are successful, they attribute that success to their own actions. When they are not successful, they blame others or factors they perceive to be out of their control. In Mindshop, we talk about this as having either an internal or external locus of control. A person with an internal locus of control takes responsibility for everything that happens to them. A person with an external locus of control often focuses on the government, the economy, global warming, or even their best friend. This type of person has a self-serving bias.

Sunk cost fallacy: When we have invested in something, we feel we should get some return on investment (ROI), and if we don't, we tend to keep pursuing that ROI no matter what. The concept of cutting one's losses is difficult to sell to someone experiencing a sunk cost fallacy. Even though a reset is required, this person will resist it.

Barriers to Personal Change

Everyone thinks of changing the world, but
no one thinks of changing himself.

— *Leo Tolstoy*

Reflecting on over forty years of consulting and coaching experience meant I could come up with a big list of potential barriers, but I decided to focus on the barriers that have been more frequently a problem over the last five years or so. I chose five barriers, only to find they were all covered adequately in the personal change success model. This included things like putting in enough effort (personal energy), the lack of a detailed plan (plan), a lack of confidence (self-confidence), inadequate tenacity (perseverance), and self-sabotage (mindset).

I was pleased that my experience validated the change model, and I decided to then look at things a little differently. For example, self-sabotage is due to mindset, but looking at it more broadly, why does it happen, and how to we put a stop to it? Another dimension that I considered was dealing with barriers to change, whatever they may be for an individual. I decided that providing a list of five barriers, while it would cover the most commonly experienced barriers, would not cover every person and his or her specific barriers. I needed a process for dealing with personal change barriers. I knew that perceived benefit was one of the nine personal change success model elements, but how can people reward themselves adequately for success in the implementation of a personal change initiative? So I had three change barrier issues to deal with: self-sabotaging behavior, removing the change barrier process, and rewarding a successful outcome of a personal change initiative.

Over thirty years ago, I became aware of some of my own self-sabotaging behavior and that of others. It was a little easier to determine why people did that when I reflected on my own behavior. I found that if I didn't feel worthy of the good things in my life, I, in effect, sent them away. I could fool others about my worthiness, but I could not fool myself. The question then became, what do I need to do to become worthier of success?

I cannot remember a specific incident where the answer came to me, but I did develop a worthiness model that could be shared with others. I named it Value To Others (VTO), and VTO became one of the five core values of the Mindshop organization. My previous book, *Value To Others,* published in 2017, provides more background on this model. The overall model for VTO can be explained as follows: the more you do for others, the higher your self-worth. The higher your self-worth, the less you sabotage yourself. The less you sabotage yourself, the more successful you will be.

Imagine a set of scales. On the left-hand side is a secret ingredient that you need to provide, and on the right-hand side are all the things that you want from life. These may include things like money, respect, family, love, and a great job. I say to people that for you to get all the things on the right-hand side of the scale, you need to put enough of the secret ingredient on the left-hand side to balance the scales. I then ask them what they think the secret ingredient is. I normally get the answer "hard work." I assume they mean that the harder you work, the more success you will get. I then make a qualifying statement: if I can think of anyone who works hard but is not successful, then hard work cannot be the answer. Both the person and I can think of plenty of examples where people worked hard but are not successful in the list of success outcomes they have listed for the right-hand side of the scale. No matter what they suggest, there are always exceptions. I then reveal and explain my answer—value to others. I then ask a secondary question: who do you think is the biggest group of people in the world that apply value to others consistently? A common answer is either the church or the Salvation Army. I acknowledge suggestions like these but remind them this is a big group, bigger than the Church or the Salvation Army. On some rare occasions, I get my answer—mothers. I remind them that mothers normally give to their children unconditionally, over a long time, often only with a short-term reward of knowing that they are doing the right thing. It is often only when their children have children that they are fully appreciated. When talking to a mother, I normally get an instant agreement to this statement!

I then ask them to think about someone in their life whom they love. The question then becomes, What do you do for them that they think is extremely valuable? Talking to a teenager still living at home, I often get the answer, "Tidy my room without being asked." For married people, the answer is commonly to do something thoughtful for their spouse. I remind them of the Pareto rule, that 20 percent of what they do for that person is creating 80 percent of the value that they are to that person, so what could they do today to double the high-value activities for that person? Making a list of things to do is never an issue.

I then ask a challenging question: so why don't you do this every day? I hear a multitude of answers including things like, "Why should I? She doesn't do it for me." My standard response then becomes that they need to take the initiative, not doing it will stop them feeling worthy of the success they so desire. I explained that it needs a big investment of value to others over a long period before enough self-worth builds up in a person. I remind them that masterpieces take time; it can be many years before the reward comes to you, and the reward will not normally come from the person that you have provided value to. It's not about them; it's all about you!

Like the example of mothers, the only short-term benefit I can guarantee you is the warm feeling from knowing that you are doing the right thing. Over time, your self-worth grows, much like a bank account; in this situation it is an emotional bank account, a bank account of value that you have provided to others. This is a bank account you can withdraw value from when you feel that you are entitled to. In the medium-term, small successes encourage you to keep going with your value-to-others strategy and behavior. In the long-term, the small successes compound into large successes. Your self-sabotaging behavior reduces, and your success becomes standard practice. Learn how to do this and a key barrier to change is removed.

If you have listed a specific barrier to change for you that is not covered by the nine personal change success model elements, then you will need a process to deal with it. The process that follows can fix almost any issue; it is simple, logical, and practical. There are only three steps to this process: mind mapping all the elements of the barrier, using the Pareto rule to identify the key elements of the mind map, and then developing specific action plans to resolve each of the key elements. Any experienced Mindshop person will be tempted to start using more powerful tools, such as a force field analysis, decision matrix, risk mitigation, or even scenario planning. I can assure you that mind map, Pareto, and action plans are more than adequate. Do not overthink it! Let me show you how this works.

Most of you will be familiar with a mind map. For those that aren't, it is simply a diagram where your specific barrier is in an ellipse in the center of the page, and then arms radiate from that ellipse, each with a specific subset of your barrier. You can keep breaking down each arm into ever increasingly more detailed factors. Following is an example of such a mind map on a hypothetical barrier—lack of skills.

Some of the key arms of the mind map include courses, training, research online, support of subject matter experts, and experience. Each of these is important, but the Pareto rule reminds us that 20 percent of them are creating 80 percent of the impact on the lack of skills barrier to change. I have put an asterisk next to those items I consider to be of most importance to solving the skills barrier. The next step is to brainstorm actions that could be used to resolve these items.

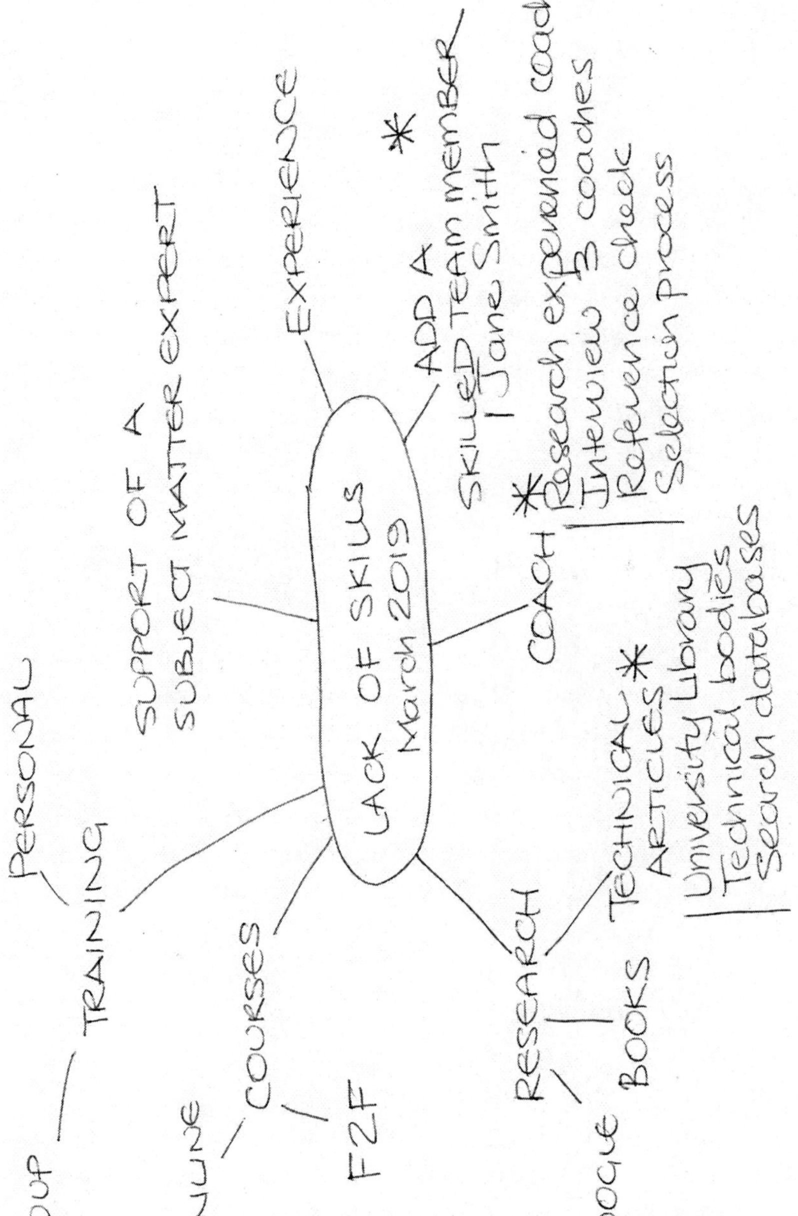
LACK OF SKILLS
March 2019
TRAINING
PERSONAL
GROUP
COURSES
ONLINE
F2F
SUPPORT OF A
SUBJECT MATTER EXPERT
EXPERIENCE
ADD A
SKILLED TEAM MEMBER
Jane Smith
*
COACH
*
Research experienced coach
Interview 3 coaches
Reference check
Selection process
RESEARCH
GOOGLE
BOOKS
TECHNICAL
ARTICLES *
University Library
Technical bodies
Search databases

On the mind map, notice how I have inserted specific actions around three of the issues. If we had twelve action items identified in this way, the final step would be to pick the three action items that would give you the biggest impact in the short term and implement those. If this doesn't give you the required boost in skills, then repeat the process and pick three different action items and apply those. You will remember that perseverance is one of our nine factors in the personal change success model. You can only fail if you stop! This process will resolve any change barrier that you choose. This means that there is nothing that can happen in your quest for personal change success that will stop you. The Mindshop tools are just structures that enable you to solve problems without overthinking them. Following the tool process will normally result in an innovative solution to your issue. The tools provide a standard approach for a team to problem solve, and it will give them confidence in their ability to develop solutions to their problems and opportunities.

Changing behavior often involves rewarding good behavior and punishing poor behavior. I think we need to avoid any plans to punish ourselves; we need to focus on rewards. We are often the last ones to consider rewarding ourselves, but what if we could share that reward with others significant to us—our family, friends, and work colleagues?

When developing a reward plan, we need to design in rewards throughout the process, as well as a major reward on completion of the plan. I made sure that both process and outcome rewards were part of my weight loss and book writing change initiatives. I felt that for both initiatives, the outcome I achieved was a significant part of the reward I received. With the weight loss initiative, my evening meal was a reward. With the book writing initiative, the rewards included sending the first draft off to my editor, getting positive feedback and constructive criticism from family members I asked to read it, and I expect to get a huge reward when I hold my first print copy in my hand in May 2019.

The outcome reward for the weight loss initiative was (believe it or not) a lunch date with my wife at a local French restaurant we both enjoy. She didn't write the book, but she supported the writing process. I write best when I'm in a quiet environment because I mostly dictate using dictation software direct into my computer. Book writing is a time-consuming undertaking spread over several months requiring a good score on each of the nine factors in the personal change success model. The outcome reward for the book writing will be a long weekend at a five-star resort (with no work commitments planned)!

I recommend that for your change initiatives, you plan for rewards that you feel add to the pleasure you get from achieving your goals, share the reward with those that have helped you along the way, and so add to your value-to-others emotional bank account. Until that level of worthiness is achieved, you may have difficulty in setting rewards that cost a lot or take a lot of time. Over the years and decades, this will become less of a problem. In the meantime, just reward yourself but make it fun!

Implementation of a Personal Change Initiative

They always say time changes things, but you actually have to change them yourself.

— Andy Warhol

There are several things to consider when you are implementing a personal change initiative that are quite different from an organizational change initiative. The obvious difference is that an organizational change initiative involves more than one person. You need others to buy into the change initiative for it to work. When you are undertaking a personal change initiative, quite often the only one you need to worry about is you. As I have already stressed, the normal probability of success with a personal change initiative is around 30 percent. I wouldn't even start working on initiatives if I felt that my success probability was as low as 30 percent. I would keep planning and working the plan so that I could 100 percent guarantee that I would have at least an 80 percent probability of success. Even then, I would think about the benefits of learning from any failures and having a second, or even third, attempt to complete my task.

This 100 percent guarantee concept is not just a mental game. To achieve this, you need to have thought of every possibility that can occur and have a plan to deal with any issues that arise. The checklist of the nine personal change success factors does most of the heavy lifting for you. The following is the process that I recommend you use to maximize your likelihood of success.

1. **Define your goal**. Your first challenge is to decide on a specific personal goal that you want to achieve. The more clarity you have around this outcome, the easier it will be to identify any barriers, determine the key issues, develop KPIs, and develop specific action plans for implementation of your solution. The outcome needs to be specific and measurable. We need to be able to tell whether we have achieved it or not.
2. **Mind map the goal**. The next step is to mind map the personal goal in as much detail as you possibly can. If you're not confident in how to do a mind map, just Google it.
3. **Pareto the mind map**. You now have a comprehensive mind map, but the problem is there's just too much information to take in, so we now Pareto that mind map. You will remember that the Pareto involves finding the 20 percent of the items on the mind map that will create 80 percent of the benefit to you of completing that outcome. The simplest way of doing this is just to put a tick or an asterisk next to the items that you think are the most important ones. Hopefully, this list of important issues is no longer than ten items, preferably just five.
4. **Brainstorm actions**. Issues may be so obvious to fix that you can simply brainstorm some action plans directly onto the mind map. More often, issues are more complex, and we need to apply extra scrutiny to be able to work out how to fix them. This is where a tool such as a force field analysis can develop action plans for you. If you are not familiar with a force field analysis, you can Google how to do it.
5. **Measure the start point**. For your specific actions, we need to somehow measure where we are now, the start point. If we don't attempt to measure the start point, we will find it difficult to

establish just how much of a difference we make through the application of our personal change initiative. In my case study of weight reduction, my start point involves measuring not only my weight but also just how much energy burning I was doing at that time. Think through all the measurements you will need to measure for the start point.

6. **Develop the one-page plan**. The control document we use for the implementation process we call a one-page plan. The one-page plan has three distinct sections, the top left is a list of bullet points describing where you are now with your project, the top right is another list of bullet points describing where you want to be at some future point with your project, and the bottom half of the plan is the list of strategies and actions that describe how we will bridge the gap between the now and the where. This is the point where you review the gaps in your Mindshop personal change success model and implement strategies and actions into your plan to address any gaps. There is little point in informing a plan with a low probability success, by ensuring that you address any gaps in the nine factors of the personal change model you can increase that probability to as high as 80 percent.
7. **Choose a buddy or coach**. It is likely that you will need some help with your personal change initiative. You will find that accountability will be enhanced if you have someone to support you. This person can be a buddy or a coach. The buddy will be well intentioned and will want you to succeed. You may lack the experience, skills, and knowledge that you need to be a success. A coach provides these essential elements.
8. **Identify and mitigate any risks**. There is one last step that I include in my personal change initiatives. I identify and then mitigate any risks that may impact on my plan. The technique I use is called failure mode and effect analysis (FMEA). List all the risks that may occur and score them each out of 10 for the severity of the risk, another 10 for the likely occurrence of that

> risk (the more likely, the higher the score), and the final 10 for my ability to detect that the risk will happen (the less visible the risk, the higher the score). I multiply three scores together to determine my risk priority number. The maximum score you can achieve is 1000. Any score over 100 I consider a problem. I then develop specific action plans to reduce my risk priority number back under 100. Can I reduce the severity, the likely occurrence, or can I improve my ability to see the risk coming? These actions then are integrated into my one-page plan.

If you follow these steps correctly, you will fix your chosen personal change initiative within an eight-week period. You are then free to select a second issue for the next eight weeks. Imagine if, every eight weeks, you could keep resolving issues for at least one year? What would your life look like at the end of that year? This is the path that I have chosen for my application of the Mindshop personal change success model.

Personal Change Q&A

He who is fixed to a star does not change his mind.

— *Leonardo da Vinci*

Having lived for almost seventy years, I have seen and experienced a lot more than many people. I consider myself personally successful, not just as a businessman, but as a citizen of the world. I am fortunate that I travel extensively for work, and I have learned firsthand how people are people in every country. My travel to China as it was opening to the West in the 1980s confirmed that. Globalization with all its challenges still produces significant opportunities for us all. The following questions are ones I remember being asked over the last year or so. Some of the questions are quite profound, and it's difficult to give succinct answers but I will do my best.

1. *Is it best to be a generalist or specialist in life?* There are two options in life: go wide and shallow or go narrow and deep. If you want to become an expert in something, then go narrow and deep. You can become an expert if you go wide and shallow, but it takes a lot more work. It is not something to be achieved with only a few years of work experience behind you. A safe approach would be to start off as a generalist; find what you love doing, throw your

whole life into it, and become a specialist. The key factor in this is to find what you love doing. To achieve this, it is far better to try lots of things without a lot of commitment rather than keep picking up and putting down shiny baubles.

2. *How do you find time to keep developing yourself?* I guess you have a choice—you either make the time, or you don't. As a student of nature, I have noticed that everything is either growing or it's dying; it cannot remain static. I have chosen to continuously grow because the alternative is not attractive. When I started my PhD training in 2006, I was already in a fifty-hour week with my work in Mindshop. I was told—and I believed—that the PhD would take around thirty hours per week over eight years. My challenge was how to find eighty hours per week. This is not normal. What you can normally do is create space; I needed to add space. I did that by working longer, going to sleep late, getting up early, working weekends, all the time supported by my wife. I have studied almost all my life because I have always been dissatisfied with how much I know. The more you learn, the more you realize you don't know. Writing this book was another example of finding time rather than creating space. You can create space by using the Pareto rule that we have mentioned a few times already. Around 20 percent of what you are currently doing is creating 80 percent of the value that you provide. This suggests that 80 percent of what you do is lower value. What can you cut out to create space? That's how you find time for personal development (and keeping fit). You cannot put more stuff into an already full vessel!
3. *Is it true that when you hit rock bottom, the only way is up?* I don't consider that I have ever been at rock bottom, but I certainly helped a lot of people who have been. There is no way of testing whether it is the true rock bottom, but if they feel it is, I can use that energy to create change for them. When they decide that they can't keep going as they are, then they are more likely to listen

to the benefits of selecting a different path. I remind them that it makes no sense to try harder at something that is not working. The only way out of such a dilemma is to try something new. Even then, they need short-term successes along the new path to encourage them to keep going. The challenge is to design the new path and to help them stay on it.

4. *In the personal change success model, some of the key factors seem to overlap, does that matter?* Think of it as a Venn diagram. There is overlap between each of the factors, some more than others. Treat each as an individual strategy; it doesn't really matter if some of the actions end up the same. You can always edit out any duplication when finalizing the plan. Keep in mind that the ten factors in the organizational change success model and the nine factors in the personal change success model are based on real data. The data is the data. The factors are the factors.
5. *I have retired, does that mean I have reached my potential?* You may have guessed that I don't intend to retire unless forced to. My retirement plan is not in place because I'm frightened to not reach my potential if I stop working. There are two key reasons why I intend to keep going: I work with my family, and my goal is to help as many people as I can in my life. These reasons, combined, seem to suggest that retirement is not for me.

   I think the modern view of retirement is to not stop cold turkey but to wind back. I would term semi-retirement as winding back to just three or four days a week. If I were forced to retire in the next twelve months, I would continue studying, researching, reading, and helping people. That means that my potential would continue to be tested. I have a view that I can get further along my development schedule if I am working for an organization than if I were retired; this is another factor why I've chosen to stay working. You need to find your own answer.
6. *What have been the most significant events in your life that helped you grow?* I have always considered that the *failures* have been the

best contributors to my skills and knowledge, whereas the *successes* have been my reward and encouragement to keep going. On that basis, then it is the failures that, in hindsight, have been the most significant contributors to my growth. That doesn't mean, of course, that I now go out looking for failures. It does mean that I want to keep looking for and tackling ever increasingly difficult issues, either problems or opportunities. I learn by stretching myself. Why not stretch myself with things that reward me at the same time?

7. *How do you suggest that I measure my progress on my personal plan?* The way I achieved this for many decades was to keep detailed journals on events that either impacted me positively or negatively. I used the journal to record my goals, my key performance indicators (KPIs), and I found that reading over them provided plenty of support for measuring my progress. I could tell that I was getting better and achieving better results. It wasn't that long ago that I decided to throw out all the journals and rely on files on my computer to set goals, develop plans, monitor KPIs, and measure my progress. The difference is that once a project is completed, I normally file it away, never to be looked at again. I get some comfort knowing it is available if I need it, but I'm not sure I whether I will ever drag it out again. Once you develop a process that automatically causes you to grow, then you can trust in that process and forget about measurement.

CONCLUSION

If we don't change, we don't grow. If we don't grow, we aren't really living.

— Gail Sheehy

Change is a constant in our lives, and one we cannot avoid. Research has indicated that the average probability of success for both organizational and personal change is around 30 percent. This means that to be successful, most people need to try to achieve their designated goal several times. This trial-and-error approach is costly in both financial and human terms. Its impact on our self-confidence and willingness to attempt change initiatives is significant. If we could be certain that our probability of success of any change initiative was at least 80 percent, then we would attempt more and succeed more.

Change is exciting. With the rapid growth rate of technology, medicines, and healthcare, together with people wishing to work longer in part because they are living longer, there is a need for new skills to deal with this extended complexity we are all experiencing. The key is to be able to differentiate between noise and substance. This book has given you the models and tools required to do just that. Unless you are extremely fortunate and won the lottery or sold a business for $150 million, you will need to continue changing and evolving to be able to fund your extended working and personal life.

Part A of this book covered the ten factors needed to ensure the 80 percent probability of success. The diagnostic provided enables you to estimate your start point on an organizational change initiative. By identifying any gaps in the ten factors required for change success, you can integrate the specific actions for these factors into your plan. Even so, there will be unexpected barriers to change, and we have covered some of the most common ones. The implementation of the change process has been described. There is even a question-and-answer section in which I have answered the most common questions asked of me by people implementing organizational change.

I have provided clarity for what to do if you are thinking about improving the profitability, growing the sales, improving the leadership, or even lifting the engagement levels of your team. The remaining challenge is to achieve equal clarity in the vision that you have for the organization. A key part of this challenge is to make sure that the rest of your team shares that vision. Team members will normally need to see where the organizational vision fits with their personal vision and career aspirations before they buy in. Therefore, we needed Part B of the book to give you equal clarity on how to best help people undertake a personal change initiative successfully.

Part B of this book covered the nine factors required to ensure success in a personal change initiative. Like the organizational change success model, the probability of success of a personal change initiative is around 30 percent. The trial-and-error approach to find an effective solution for a personal issue is also costly in terms of time, money, self-confidence, and willingness to change.

The nine factors that form part of the personal change success model enable you to lift the 30 percent probability of success to an acceptable minimum of 80 percent probability. If a person believes that the probability is this high, then he or she is likely to engage in the change process. Once I developed the model in early 2019, I was able to apply in eight-week cycles solutions to my personal issues and opportunities, starting with regaining control of my weight. If you want to control your weight, lift your fitness level, improve a relationship, control your spending, further your education, or even improve your career, then the nine steps will help you do any of these. Once you have a draft plan in place, all you need to do is to measure the gaps in the nine factors using the diagnostic provided for personal change success and develop specific actions to maximize your score in each section of readiness, capability, and beliefs.

As in Part A, Part B of the book lists the likely barriers to change, provides a personal change implementation process, and answers some frequently asked questions. All these resources arm you with everything you need to successfully complete a personal change initiative. The same resource can be used to help family, friends, and work colleagues if they are ready to listen to your advice. You cannot force change on people, but if they are asking you to help, knowing that you have an evidence-based, proven model and implementation process for personal change will give you the confidence to offer support.

If change is a constant in life, then it makes sense that we arm ourselves with best-practice resources and processes to maximize our probability of success. If you are experiencing a Groundhog Day, or even a groundhog year or two, then you are ready to consider making step changes in your organization or in your personal life. I hope you find my research, model, and suggestions for implementation helpful. I wish you well and success in life.

ACKNOWLEDGEMENTS

Sometimes if you want to see a change for the better,
you have to take things into your own hands.

— *Clint Eastwood*

There are many people whom I need to acknowledge, and just because I mention some and not others does not mean I don't appreciate everyone who has touched my life. Every experience has been invaluable irrespective of whether, at the time, I perceived it as helpful or hindering. We are all the sum of all our experiences and our potential.

The first group of people that comes to mind to thank is my immediate family. This is because of their support but also specifically some of them read through my first draft and offered valuable insights and comments. Sometimes I labored a point and other times I probably did not fully explain myself, but they were quick to point out these opportunities. As normal for me, I needed the feedback quickly to meet my schedule, and, like all Masons, they were responsive.

There were many people involved in the two research programs conducted to produce data that enabled the development of the two change success models described in this book. The first study in 2014 required around 250 people to achieve the data required; the second study in 2019 required 40 people. I formally thank these people for sharing their knowledge and experiences to help others. There was an additional group of people that were significant. They were the primarily Mindshop people who were taught the two models, provided insightful feedback, and then tested the models in the field with their own clients. Their faith in our research and trust in their own abilities to apply the models say a lot about their own values and standards.

My source of the quotations at the start of each chapter mostly came from one organization; their website is www.brightdrops.com. I thank them for the use of their collection of quotes around the change topic.

The final group of people to thank are the readers. This is my second book; the first was titled *Value To Others* and was published in 2017. It is no coincidence that *Change Success* was published in 2019. One of my key goals is to write a book at the start of every second year from now on. I want to help as many people as I can indefinitely. The best way to do this is to publish and improve the quality and content of my books every time I write a new one. Thank you for being patient in my authoring development process. If you would like to give me feedback on how to do this better I can be reached at cmason@mindshop.com

ABOUT CHRIS MASON

When you are through changing, you are through.

— *Bruce Barton*

When authors draft a list of achievements for the readers of the book that they have written, it is normally to provide context for their book and their views, suggestions, and experiences shared with the readers. In this case, there are two related but distinct books within the one cover. Part A of this book is about organizational change success, whereas Part B covers personal change success. They are related because organizations are comprised of people undergoing personal change. The culture of an organization is really the sum of the beliefs and behaviors of every employee within that organization.

I'm a person before I am a leader of an organization, so I will cover my personal achievements first. I am a husband to Julie for 47 years in 2019, father to three remarkable children whom I work with, as well as being in the same family, (in birth order) James, Brett, and Emily. There are some equally remarkable spouses to my children and then six grandchildren. Julie and my extended family are mostly based in Adelaide, South Australia, and we have a global network of friends. My clients, who are also mostly friends, are global, currently spanning eleven distinct countries. I am thankful for my health and happiness and the fact that I have not been given too many personal issues to contend with; I reserve my energy for helping others.

On the business side, I am founder and chairman of Mindshop; a director of a second family business, Traction IT; a long-term director of a large HVAC company, AG Coombs; and a director of the charitable trust sponsored by Mindshop called Mindshop Excellence. My background is an integration of technical and administrative organizations in electrical, pulp and paper, employer organization, and laser technology, as well as everything listed above. This probably means that I am a jack-of-all-trades and master of none, but it has been useful to be a generalist rather than a specialist. My current role is primarily as a coach of leaders. I help develop best-practice resources that these leaders can use to continuously improve their organizations. Aged seventy in 2019, my vision is to be still working as I reach my nineties. To achieve that and still be of relevance, I need to be on a continuous learning process where my skills and knowledge lead, or at least match, the needs of my clients. There are many people who cannot be part of the Mindshop organization, and my books are designed, in part, as a mechanism to help them. Anywhere in the world when I walk past a business or an organization, I feel slightly guilty that I am not stopping to help their leaders. I mitigate that guilt by training hundreds of Mindshop people each year, documenting my knowledge so it can reach thousands, and then supporting those who can help the leaders of any business that needs it.

Made in United States
North Haven, CT
06 November 2026

21866984R00092